MEENA PATHAK'S
COMPLETE
INDIAN
COOKING

MEENA PATHAK'S
COMPLETE
INDIAN
COOKING

NEW HOLLAND

Published in 2009 by
New Holland Publishers Ltd.
London • Cape Town • Sydney • Auckland

86–88 Edgware Road, London W2 2EA, United Kingdom
www.newhollandpublishers.com

80 McKenzie Street, Cape Town 8001, South Africa

Unit 1, 66 Gibbes Street, Chatswood, NSW 2067, Australia

218 Lake Road, Northcote, Auckland, New Zealand

ISBN 978 1 84773 159 3

Senior Editor: Clare Sayer
Patak's Development Chef: Sunil Menon
Design: Roger Hammond
Photographer: John Freeman
Assistant photographer: Alex Dow
Stylist: Labeena Ishaque
Production: Hazel Kirkman
Editorial Direction: Rosemary Wilkinson

Reproduction by Pica Digital PTE Ltd., Singapore
Printed and bound in Times Offset (M) Sdn. Bhd., Malaysia

10 9 8 7 6 5 4 3

Contents

Introduction

I can't remember when I first became interested in cooking, since it now seems like second nature. I do know however, that food has always been a great passion of mine. Some of my earliest and best memories are of going to the market with my grandmother in Bombay (now called Mumbai) and watching her haggle to get the best produce! I was always fascinated in the kitchen and so was gradually allowed to help more and more. By the age of ten, therefore, I was happily going to the market myself and helping to cook meals for the family. I grew up in Bombay but I was lucky enough to be able to spend holidays with my parents wherever my family were based at the time (as my father was in the army). This led to extensive travelling, and so, in time, I learnt about the many regional differences that exist throughout India and I soon discovered a whole new world of ingredients, flavours and recipes.

It is important to me to emphasise that everyone can cook good Indian food for themselves on an everyday basis. Most of us (myself included) simply don't have the time to spend long hours in the kitchen and we also want to use ingredients that are readily available in the shops. It's important too that food should be as naturally healthy as possible, keeping an eye on the levels of fat. The busy lifestyles we live and our desire for healthy food does mean that I have had to adapt some classic Indian dishes to make them easier to prepare: I believe there is always time for good delicious food and it doesn't always have to be unhealthy. My love of spices is always at the heart of my cooking and I love experimenting with different flavours, using influences from other cuisines as well as from India.

This collection of recipes brings together some of my favourite recipes, for snacks, casual lunches or big celebrations. I hope you enjoy cooking them and, of course, eating them!

Meera Pathak

India's culinary traditions

INDIA, my homeland, is a vast subcontinent which is made up of several states, all with their own unique cookery traditions and tastes. India has a multi-layered culture, with a population of one billion, five major faiths, numerous languages and dialects and a rich heritage. Indian food is a reflection of this heritage and is shaped by the culture and religious beliefs of the people. The regionality of the cuisine is also affected by the vastly differing landscapes which influence what can be grown. The climate is also a factor – in the colder northern states, warming, aromatically spiced dishes are eaten, whereas in the intense heat of southern India, the food is lighter and uses more coconut and black pepper.

The regions of India

I only began to appreciate the diversity of the regions of India when I started travelling in my summer holidays, visiting the places where my father, who was in the army, was posted. I remember visiting an army camp in the far north of India and catching my first glimpse of the snow-capped peaks of the Himalayan mountain range. The breathtaking valley of Kashmir has lush meadows and is where India's saffron is grown. Its lakes are beautiful and sailing on the famous Dal lake is a truly romantic experience. It is cool enough to rear sheep, which is why lamb or mutton is used extensively in Kashmiri dishes and this is where I had my first taste of meat. Apple and apricot orchards dot the countryside and black cumin seeds grow wild. The world-famous basmati rice grows in the foothills of the Himalayas. The soil here is fertile and irrigated by the phosphorous-rich waters of the Ganges – the river is icy cold but if you're brave enough for a quick dip it is wonderfully refreshing.

The state of Punjab in the northwest is one of the most fertile, due to the fact that it is irrigated by five major rivers. Although rice does grow here, the staple diet is wheat. Travelling through Punjab you come across tiny villages where the food is still cooked in earthenware pots over open fires. The food from Punjab has become very popular in restaurants abroad – the classic dishes such as tandooris, tikkas, naan and lassi all come from Punjab. The best food can be found in small roadside restaurants where the menu is basic but the food is delicious and fresh. A regional specialty is Kaali dal, made from black urad dal and kidney beans slowly simmered with cinnamon, garlic and cloves. The only accompaniment you need is some bread and a large glass of freshly churned lassi.

To the east, lie the fertile plains of Bengal. The coastal area is lined with coconut palms and the fields covered with mustard plantations. An abundance of fish is eaten in this region. My travels also took me north of Bengal to the sloping tea plantations in the Assam hills where the cool air and seasonal rains make the climate ideal for growing the famous Darjeeling tea.

This page and opposite: **The sights of India are often breathtaking and this vibrancy is reflected in Indian cooking. Colours are everywhere, from traditionally decorated trucks to the day's catch in Cochin to lush tea plantations in Kerala.**

To the west lies the Malabar coast and this is the area that I associate with home. My family originally came from Gujarat but I grew up in my grandmother's house in Bombay (now called Mumbai), the cosmopolitan capital of Maharashtra. Goa, to the south, is where I spent many holidays as a teenager, eating my entire quota of fish cooked with spices and coconut, and drinking feni, a drink made from cashew nuts. Gujarat, Maharashtra and Goa are all strikingly different but I was lucky living in Bombay where I could experience the contrasts. The Deccan plateau is in the heart of Maharashtra and the cotton for our clothes was grown in the cotton fields here. On visits to my aunt's sugarcane plantation we used to stop and pick peanuts off the trees and see the millet and barley being harvested – if we were lucky we would catch the sounds of local workers singing folk songs as they worked.

South India is lush and green with a maze of small rivers. Food here is very different to that cooked in the rest of India. Rice and fish are the staples, while flavours such as curry leaves, black pepper, asafoetida and coconut are fundamental to most south Indian dishes.

Influences from abroad

Though India is one of the oldest civilisations it has been enriched over the centuries by other invading cultures. The most important is probably the Mughal invasion in the sixteenth century. This had a profound effect on the country and its cuisine. The Muslim conquerors brought their favourite dishes and cooking methods to the north Indian states and the fusion of these with Indian staples and local foods led to the evolution of Mughlai cuisine. Meat was introduced and transformed into delicate kormas, spicy kebabs and fragrant biryanis. However, the influence was concentrated mainly in the north. This is because it was relatively easy to invade the north via the Khyber Pass and also because the northern states enjoyed a similar climate to the invaders' home countries. South India was seen as relatively isolated and because of this, it has remained predominantly vegetarian.

The Parsis arrived in India in the seventh century after fleeing religious persecution in Iran, and settled on the coast of Gujarat. The Parsi community remains a small one, for they pledged not to spread their religion or to intermarry. They have nonetheless contributed significantly to Indian culture and I have included some of my favourite Parsi dishes in this book.

The Portuguese were the first colonisers of India in 1498 and the last to leave in 1961 and their mark has most certainly been left on the cuisine of Goa, where they arrived. Fish is a favourite, as well as pork vindaloo, a Goan signature dish famous for its searing heat.

The influence of religion on food

Although more than 80 per cent of Indians are Hindu, there are several other important religions. Muslims account for about 12 per cent of the population, the remainder being Christians, Buddhists and Parsis. In Hinduism there are five main castes. Each has different food taboos and customs but in the broadest sense, all Hindus avoid eating beef as the cow is considered sacred in Indian mythology. Certain Hindus are strict vegetarians, which means they avoid fish, shellfish and eggs as well as meat and poultry.

Some very strict vegetarians won't eat tomatoes or watermelon because their colour resembles that of meat. However, many middle class Hindus eat meat in restaurants and non-Hindu homes. The Bengali Hindus will eat sacrificial meat and fish.

Muslims make up a sizeable part of the population and from this community come most Indian meat dishes. They have some forbidden foods, most notably pork. Alcohol is also forbidden though some Muslims bend the rules.

Indian Christians have virtually no food taboos but some avoid meat on Fridays and cut back on certain foods during Lent. Perhaps the most restrictive diet belongs to the Jains, who practise ultra-vegetarianism. That can make life very difficult for the cook!

Fasting and feasting

There are over 20 major feast days in the Hindu calendar and probably as many fast days. People fast on special days for different gods. Rather than avoiding all food, fasting involves taking a vow of self-denial. However, there are certain foods that are very definitely forbidden on these days, for example, meat, alcohol and, in certain regions, rice. The whole process is quite complicated because of the regional differences. As a child I used to think of the food cooked on those fasting days as celebration food. Though

Above, left to right: **Garlands made of flowers are often part of the prayer ritual; traditional Kathakali dancers in Cochin; women collecting water from a standpipe in Chennai.**

we did not 'fast' we wanted to eat the food cooked for those who were fasting. The food for fasting days includes nuts, potatoes, fruits, certain vegetables, sago, milk, yogurt, paneer, coconut and root vegetables. Food would always be cooked in ghee during fasting. In very strict families the kitchen is washed clean before the food is cooked, and a small prayer ceremony is conducted before the meal is eaten.

There are hundreds of reasons to celebrate in India, whether it is a harvest celebration, a god's day or a special date in the Hindu calendar. Food plays an important part in these celebrations, along with gifts and prayers. The most widely celebrated festival is Diwali, the Festival of Lights, which takes place every year in October or November. It is the beginning of the Hindu New Year and is a time when a lot of festive food is prepared, particularly desserts. The preparations start a month in advance and many Indians spring-clean their houses to symbolise a new beginning. It's a time for reflection and charity. It is also the beginning of the financial year, so you might pray to the goddess of wealth or make offerings of silver and gold.

Foods for healing

For centuries Indians have believed that food should be eaten not only for taste but also to help cure physical and mental ailments. Ayurveda is the science of diet, healing and health. It is the most widely practised form of medicine in India and many Indian cooks have an instinct for what ingredients to add to a dish to help alleviate certain problems. Increasingly, this way of eating is being explored in other parts of the world. Food plays an important part in our lives and therefore the chemical balance provided by what we eat aids healing and promotes good health and well-being.

Ayurvedic healers believe there are six basic tastes – sweet, sour, salty, pungent, bitter and astringent – and each of these tastes helps in healing specific problems.

Sweet	soothing, nourishing, energising and satisfying
Sour	increases appetite, helps digestion, produces saliva
Salty	increases water intake, gives the skin a glow, cures stiffness
Pungent	increases blood circulation, kills worms in the upper and lower digestive tracts, purifies the mouth
Bitter	blood purifier, firms the skin and is an antidote to poison
Astringent	aids digestion, blood purifier.

The following foods and spices are believed to help alleviate certain conditions:

■ **Black cumin, fish, eggs, figs, sesame seeds, sweet potatoes, mangoes, ghee, sago**
Help subdue wind in the body
■ **Buttermilk, cucumber, courgettes, lemons, oranges, radish, spinach, water, sunflower seeds**
Help subdue bile in the body
■ **Dates, alcohol, aubergines, fenugreek, ginger, honey, onions, tea, salt, pickles, lentils**

My favourite ingredients

Ajowan (ajwain)

Ajowan seeds are very similar in appearance to cumin seeds and have a strong, distinctive flavour that resembles aniseed. The spice is used to add a zing to many fish and vegetable dishes as well as some flour-based snacks. Chewed on their own, ajowan seeds may help alleviate stomach-ache as well as diarrhoea and colic. The spice comes from a herbaceous plant closely related to caraway which has feathery leaves, flowers and tiny seeds. These seeds, when dried, are the spice.

Asafoetida (hing)

Asafoetida has a very overpowering, almost unpleasant smell, which is calmed when it is fried in oil. It is often added to dals to alleviate wind. Asafoetida is made from a dried gum resin which is taken from the roots of a perennial plant native to Kashmir. The dried resin is ground to a yellowish powder which is used in small quantities in cooking in many lentil and vegetable dishes.

Aubergine (baingan or brinjal)

Aubergines are the fruits of a plant originally cultivated in India but now grown in warm climates throughout the world. They come in all different shapes, colours and sizes, from deep purple, green or even white-skinned ones. They are always eaten cooked and can be made into a hot pickle, sliced and deep-fried for a tasty snack, or made into a spicy curry.

Bay leaf (tej patta)

These are the leaves of the evergreen bay tree, used in Indian cooking in their dried form. The leaves are generally added to hot oil at the beginning of a dish to release their sweet, delicate aroma.

Cardamom (elaichi)

Cardamom has a delicate, aromatic fragrance, which is used to flavour meat and vegetable dishes as well as desserts and drinks. It is an essential ingredient in garam masala (see page 22). Cardamom is the dried fruit of a plant native to India. It takes the form of a pod containing brown seeds, which can be ground to a fine powder or used whole. You can also use cracked whole pods in cooking. There are several varieties and you will see brown cardamom pods as well as the pale green ones but the green ones have a much finer flavour.

Cassia (jungli dalchini)

Often confused with cinnamon, cassia bark is harder and coarser and with an inferior flavour. It is used in much the same way as cinnamon.

Chat masala

Chat masala is a spice mix, usually made with salt and pepper, cumin seeds, ground ginger and dried mango. Look out for it in Asian grocers.

Chillies, dried (lal mirch)

There are a confusing number of chilli varieties but the most commonly used dried chillies in Indian cooking are the small, red ones – they will add a fiery heat to any dish. They can be used whole, crushed, flaked or in powdered form. Remove the seeds before using to lessen the heat.

Chillies, fresh (hari mirch)

I generally use the long thin green chillies when fresh ones are called for, although they can vary in heat so use with caution. The seeds can be removed to make them less fiery. They form an essential part of many pastes, including the one given on page 20. Always wash your hands after handling chillies.

Cinnamon (dalchini)

The spice used in cooking is the dried inner bark of the cinnamon tree, an evergreen native to Sri Lanka. It is one of the most important and earliest known spices and is an essential ingredient of garam masala. It is used in its 'stick' form as well as a ground spice and its warm, sweet aroma enhances rice dishes, as well as meat dishes and desserts. In Ayurvedic medicine, it is used to alleviate headaches, colds and rheumatic pains. Cinnamon bark infused in hot water is a soothing drink for a sore throat.

Cloves (long)

Cloves are the small, dried buds of the clove tree, which have a sweet aroma but a bitter taste. They are used to flavour rice and savoury dishes and are also used in spice mixtures, including garam masala.

Above: **A vegetable seller displays an array of produce, including tomatoes, okra, aubergines, tapioca and beans.**

Coconut (narial)

Coconut palms grow in abundance all over southern India. The white flesh is used fresh or desiccated, either as a garnish or in chutneys and pastes. Creamed coconut is used as a base for curries, and coconut milk is used in both sweet and savoury dishes. Its delicate flavour enhances fish and chicken curries as well as vegetable dishes. Do not keep desiccated coconut for more than a month, as it will eventually go rancid. Coconut milk can be bought in cans, as powder or in block form (reconsitute with water). Coconut water, the liquid inside coconuts, is used mainly for drinks.

Coriander, fresh
(hara dhaniya)
Fresh green coriander is used as a herb and has quite a different aroma to the dried seeds. It makes a wonderful garnish and will lift a dish both visually and in flavour. Generally, recipes usually call for only the leaves to be used but I use the stalks wherever I can – they are great thrown into soups and sauces.

Coriander seeds (dhaniya)
The pungent, slightly sweet, citrus flavour of coriander seeds is used in vegetable, meat, fish and poultry dishes. The seeds come from a leafy herb bearing lacy flowers – these seeds are dried and used extensively, whole or ground, as an aromatic spice in Indian cooking. The whole seeds are often dry-roasted and then coarsely crushed with other spices to make a spice mixture. The flavour of the ground spice is not as intense as that of whole seeds.

Cumin (jeera)
The distinctive aroma of cumin seeds is used to flavour rice and curries. Cumin seeds are the fruits of a small annual herb, which grows throughout India. They are used dried and range in colour from light, greenish brown to dark brown. They can be fried in hot oil to intensify their flavour or dry-roasted and then ground with other spices. Ready-ground cumin is available from supermarkets but it quickly loses its flavour. Another variety of cumin is black cumin (kala jeera), although black cumin is less aromatic and not as bitter in flavour.

Curry leaves (kari patta)
This aromatic herb is used to add flavour to many dishes, particularly in southern India, but it also has medicinal properties and can ease stomach pains. Despite its name, it has no flavour of curry and is actually related to the lemon family. Curry leaves are fried in hot oil which brings out their nutty flavour. They are readily available in Asian grocers and are best used fresh as dried curry leaves have only a fraction of the flavour. I often freeze curry leaves; first wash them and then dry them on tea towels. Then simply put them into a bag and place in the freezer. They will lose some of their colour but none of the flavour.

Fennel seeds (saunf)
Dried fennel seeds are used throughout India, not only to add a sweet, aniseed flavour to a variety of dishes, but also as a mouth freshener. They are similar in appearance to cumin seeds though greener in colour. Fennel is used as a digestive aid and is also thought to relieve wheezing, catarrh and asthma.

Fenugreek (methi)
Fenugreek is used to flavour a variety of dishes and is also used in bread making. It is one of the most powerful and ancient spices, believed to aid digestion. It grows as an annual plant in the north of India and its leaves are used both fresh and dried. The dried seeds are small, hard and yellowish and have a pungent aroma – they are commonly used in ground spice mixes. Dried fenugreek leaves are often referred to as kasoori methi.

Flour
Indians use a variety of flours for cooking, the most common being wheat flour, which is used to make chapattis and other breads such as parathas, puris and rotis. Chickpea flour, also known as gram flour or besan, is also used extensively. It is a dull yellow colour and has an earthy aroma and is much finer than wheat flour. Its rich, nutty taste is ideal for making light batters for fried snacks, such as pakoras and bhajias. It is also stirred into curries to thicken them. Water chestnut flour is often used in the preparation of snacks, particularly in Kashmir, where the singhara nut, a variety of water chestnut, is dried and ground to a flour.

Garam masala

Garam masala is a blend of spices – garam means 'hot' or 'aromatic' and masala means 'mix'. The spices and quantities used vary enormously from region to region and even from house to house – most cooks will boast their own very special blend, while keeping the exact ingredients a closely guarded secret. The spices can be ground coarsely or to a fine powder which is usually sprinkled over a dish towards the end of the cooking time to release its aroma. There is no definitive recipe for garam masala but see page 22 for my preferred recipe, as well as some regional variations.

Garlic (lahsun)

Garlic is a hardy, bulbous member of the onion family. The bulb consists of a number of cloves encased in a thin papery covering. It has a long history and is believed to have great curative powers, from aiding digestion to helping guard against infectious diseases. It has an unmistakable aroma and is eaten throughout India except by some Kashmiri Hindus and the Jain sect. In Indian cooking it is most commonly used as a pulp and fried with ginger and onion in oil as a base in many recipes, particularly meat dishes. See page 18 for my tips on preparing garlic.

Ginger (adrak)

Ginger has a pungent, fresh aroma and has been prescribed for many ailments – a ginger infusion is great for a sore throat or cold, while I use it to cure travel sickness and nausea. It is the underground root or rhizome of a herbaceous plant grown throughout Asia. In its fresh state it is most often used as a pulp – the outer skin can be removed and the fibrous flesh is either finely chopped or pulped (see page 18) and used to impart a distinct flavour to a variety of dishes. Dried ginger is also available as a ground spice which can be used to flavour drinks as well as savoury and sweet dishes.

Gourd, bitter (karela)

The term gourd is applied loosely to some vegetables in the curcubit family, which encompasses pumpkins, both winter and summer squash, cucumbers and melons. Bitter gourds or karela are native to India and have a green knobbly skin. I use them in spicy curries and dals (see page 90).

Gourd, bottle (doodhi)

Bottle gourd or doodhi is a wonderful vegetable which is great used in dals and spicy vegetable dishes (see page 108). It is long and marrow-shaped with a hard, pale green skin and sweet white flesh.

Jaggery (gur)

Jaggery is a dark, sticky, fudge-like sugar which is made from sugar cane juice that has been boiled down. It has a distinct, musky flavour and is used to sweeten a whole range of dishes. Brown sugar can be substituted although it won't have quite the same sweet richness.

Lentils and pulses (dal)

The word 'dal' means lentils or pulses and is often used to describe a lentil-based dish. Pulses are an excellent source of protein and dal is a staple throughout India, particularly in the Punjab. There are countless different varieties but some of the most common ones are channa dal (white gram lentils), toover dal (yellow lentils), masoor dal (red lentils) and urad dal (black gram lentils). Dal is also used to describe chickpeas and red kidney beans.

Mango (aam)

Mangoes are widely cultivated throughout India and are used in cooking in both their ripe and unripe (green) states. Fresh mangoes are used in desserts and drinks and are rich in vitamin C. Mango chutneys and pickles are a firm favourite and are often highly spiced, while mango powder (amchoor) is dried ground mango which is used as a spice to give a sweet-and-sour flavour to snacks and lentil dishes.

Mint (pudhina)

This fresh herb is not used extensively in Indian cooking but it does appear in recipes for chutneys and dips and in some specific meat and chicken dishes such as Minced lamb with peas and mint (see page 68).

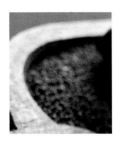

Mustard seeds (rai)

Round in shape and sharp tasting, mustard seeds are used to flavour a variety of dishes. Whole black mustard seeds are often thrown into hot oil or 'popped' at the beginning of a recipe – this gives them a sweet, nutty taste that enhances vegetables, pulses, fish dishes and relishes. The mustard plant is an annual which bears bright yellow flowers. The seeds of the plant, when dried, are the spice. There are three types of mustard seeds, of which brown and black are the most widely used in India.

Nutmeg and mace
(jaiphal/javitri)

Nutmeg and mace come from the same tree, mace being the lacy outer covering of the nutmeg kernel. Nutmeg has a warm, sweet flavour and is used in small quantities in desserts, often grated from a whole nutmeg. It is also used in some garam masala mixes. Mace is similar in flavour but is not as sweet and is more often used as a ground spice. Nutmeg is widely used in Indian medicine and is believed to help overcome bronchitis and rheumatism.

Oil and ghee

Indians cook with a variety of oils. Groundnut or sunflower oil is most commonly used for starting off dishes and is also used for deep-frying. Coconut oil, with its strong aroma, is used more in the south, while the dark yellow mustard oil is used extensively in Bengal in fish dishes. Ghee is clarified butter and many Indian recipes use ghee as the cooking fat. It can be heated to very high temperatures without burning and does not require refrigeration. In most cases oil can be substituted for ghee and increasingly Indians are using the lighter vegetable oils as a healthier alternative.

Okra (bhendi)

Okra are the edible pods of an annual plant that grows in tropical and subtropical regions. The pods are typically ridged and contain small seeds and a sticky substance – however if you carefully wash and dry the okra before cooking you can prevent them going sticky. Okra is delicious when prepared as a dry vegetable dish (see page 88).

Paneer

Paneer is a fresh Indian cheese made with curdled milk, originally introduced by the Mughal invaders. It quickly became a favourite dish in the north but it is now eaten all over India. It doesn't have a great deal of flavour but it does have a wonderful firm texture and will take on other flavours during cooking. For vegetarians, it is also an excellent source of protein. It is often cubed and lightly fried until golden brown before being added to other ingredients. It holds its shape well and will not crumble during cooking. You can make your own, but good-quality paneer is much more readily available now so I would not recommend you go to the trouble of making it.

Pepper (kalamiri)

Pepper is the most commonly used spice and is sometimes known as the King of Spices. It is the fruit of a perennial vine which bears berries or peppercorns. The black, white, red and green varieties all come from same plant – the difference in colour occurs in the way they are processed. Black pepper is made by drying green peppercorns in the sun while white pepper is made when ripe berries are softened in water, hulled and then dried. In India, I used to pickle green peppercorns in brine – it's often used as a pickle in the winter months.

Poppy seeds (khus khus)

Indian poppy seeds are a pale ivory colour and are used in cooking in a variety of ways – they can be ground with other spices to thicken sauces for meat and fish and they are also used in sweet dishes and drinks. Poppy seeds come from the annual flowering plant, also known for its narcotic properties.

Rice

Rice is one of the main staples of Indian food but is much more fundamental to the southern diet, whereas in northern India, bread is more commonly eaten as an accompaniment. In the south, you are likely to eat rice at every meal, from uttapam for breakfast to sweet rice puddings. Long-grain white rice is the most common but there are countless varieties, from Kerala's red rice to the sticky rice of Assam. I always recommend using basmati rice as its aromatic flavour is far superior to other varieties.

Saffron (kesar)

Saffron is considered the most expensive spice in the world and is worth its weight in gold. It is actually made from the stigmas of the crocus flower, which are hand picked and dried in the sun. A gift of saffron is something very special and it is often exchanged at Diwali. Saffron, which is sold as strands and as a powder, is used in very small quantities to flavour both savoury and sweet dishes.

Tamarind (imli)

The tamarind tree is evergreen and bears long, crescent-shaped pods. Within these pods are the seeds, surrounded by a fleshy pulp. It is this pulp, with its fruity sweet-and-sour aroma, that is used in Indian cooking. It appears in a number of south Indian and Gujarati lentil dishes and can be made into a wonderful sweet chutney (see page 111). According to Ayurvedic medicine, it is beneficial as a mild laxative, and tamarind water is often recommended to soothe a sore throat.

Turmeric (haldi)

Although used mainly for colour, this spice imparts a subtle flavour and is also used extensively for its antiseptic and digestive properties. Turmeric is the root, or rhizome, of a herbaceous perennial plant related to the ginger family. This bright yellow, bitter-tasting spice is sold ground although the small roots are also available fresh or dried. Like ginger, it needs to be peeled and ground before using. If your hands become stained when preparing fresh turmeric, you can clean them by rubbing them with potato peelings. Stains on work surfaces or crockery can be removed by covering them with bicarbonate of soda and washing-up liquid. Leave for about 20 minutes and then rinse off.

My useful cooking tips

Cooking authentic Indian food can seem daunting to many cooks but it doesn't have to be that way – trust me! When I first came to live in England, many of the herbs and spices and other specialist ingredients were hard to find, but now they are readily available in good supermarkets and Asian grocers.

One of the things that I hear over and over is that the ingredients lists in Indian recipes are too long and many people think that this means that they have to spend a lot of time preparing ingredients. I've been cooking almost all my life, and with a family to feed (which often means extended family), I have learnt a few tricks on saving time – without compromising on flavour. So, whether you are preparing ingredients in advance, storing spices and herbs or making fresh pulps and pastes, follow my advice and you will soon find that you are cooking authentic Indian food without any hassle.

As you look through the recipes in this book you will see that some ingredients appear often and form the basis for many dishes. Garlic, ginger, onions and coriander are used extensively in Indian cooking, along with certain spices and herbs. Buying and preparing these from scratch every time you want to cook an Indian dish can be time-consuming and laborious so here are some ideas and tips to help you on your way.

Garlic

A large number of my recipes call for garlic pulp. One large clove will make about ¹/₂ teaspoon of garlic pulp. You can prepare it in batches and keep it for later. Simply peel the garlic cloves and purée in a food processor or blender with a little water until you have a smooth pulp. This will keep in airtight containers in the refrigerator for up to ten days and can be used as necessary. If you want to be really organised, you can freeze garlic pulp in ice cube trays kept specifically for this purpose. Once frozen, remove from the trays and store in the freezer in airtight containers.

Fresh ginger

Exactly the same principle applies to ginger pulp, which is also a basic ingredient in many of my recipes. Simply peel the tough outer skin with a small sharp knife and roughly chop the ginger into small pieces. Purée the pieces in a food processor or blender with a little water until you have a smooth consistency. Again, you can store this in the refrigerator in airtight containers or freeze as above. However, I never like to waste anything so I usually leave my ginger unpeeled as there is a lot of flavour in the skin. Wash the ginger root well and soak it for a few minutes in warm water to remove any dirt in the crevices. When I do decide to peel it I keep the peelings and add them to a cup of hot water for a soothing ginger infusion.

Preparing ginger

Onions

Onions are used in Indian cooking in many different ways – to flavour, colour, thicken or garnish dishes. If onions are being used to make a rich sauce for a meat dish they are usually fried slowly in oil or ghee. You can fry batches of sliced onions in advance and keep them in the refrigerator in airtight containers for up to two weeks. I use raw onions to season new cast-iron pans – simply cut an onion in half, wrap it in a piece of muslin or similar thin cloth so you can hold it easily, dip into oil and then rub the cut side over the surface of a hot pan until it sizzles and starts to smell nicely of burnt onion. Remove from the heat and wipe off the excess oil with a piece of absorbent kitchen paper.

Using and storing fresh herbs

The most commonly used fresh herb in Indian cooking is coriander. It is used as a basis for green chutneys, as an ingredient in many vegetable and chicken dishes and, of course, as a fragrant and colourful garnish for a whole range of dishes. When chopped fresh coriander is called for, most people usually just use the leaves, but I like to use the stalks of the plant as well wherever I can – they are full of flavour and are great in soups and stocks. Fresh coriander can quickly lose its flavour but you can freeze it by washing the leaves well, leaving them to dry completely on a tea towel and then freezing in sealed plastic bags. It can then be used in cooking, although not as a garnish. Other fresh herbs such as fenugreek leaves and curry leaves can be stored in this way.

Many recipes, particularly those from southern India, call for fried curry leaves as a garnish. You can prepare these in advance: simply fry them in hot oil for 2–3 minutes. Remove from the pan with a slotted spoon, drain on absorbent kitchen paper and, when cool, store in an airtight container for up to ten days.

Spice pastes

Pastes form a very important part of Indian cooking. The one I have included here is a classic combination of flavours which is used to spice a number of dishes, especially vegetables such as okra, aubergine and beans. One of my first memories is of watching our cook at home in India making this paste with a cylindrical crusher on a flat stone. He would place a clean cloth under this very heavy stone and sit with a bowl with all the ingredients mixed together. Working with a small amount at a time, he would crush the ingredients into a paste, occasionally sprinkling the stone with water. Most Indian households have their own basic masala and, once you understand the principle of blending ingredients together, you can play around with the ingredients to make your own version. Traditionally, this would be made fresh every day but it will keep for five to six days if stored in a refrigerator.

Coriander, chilli, garlic and ginger paste

(Makes about 12 tablespoons)
8–10 dried red chillies
6 cloves garlic, peeled
5 cm (2 in) fresh root ginger, chopped
2 large bunches fresh coriander, stalks and leaves, chopped
6–8 fresh curry leaves
1 tablespoon sea salt
2 tablespoons green chillies, chopped

The simplest way to make this paste is to place all the ingredients together in a food processor or blender and process to a smooth paste. Add 2–3 tablespoons of water as you blend to make a smooth consistency. Store in the refrigerator in an airtight container for up to six days.

Using and storing dried spices

Spices are an important part of Indian culture – and not just because they are used extensively in the cooking. Many of the spices that we use today have been part of Ayurvedic medicine for thousands of years and some are highly revered for their special powers (see pages 12–17 for more information on individual spices). However, it is food that we are concerned with here. If you are new to cooking Indian food you may find the range of spices daunting but once you have grasped the basics of how spices work and what the most common flavour combinations are, you will soon be able to experiment and flavour your dishes to your own liking. An expert Indian cook knows instinctively how to mix and match certain flavours, when to add a little bit of something or other, and what is missing from a spice mixture. With my help you will begin to discover the secrets of using spices!

As you look through the recipes you will discover that there is a certain order of cooking. There are spices that are always used at the beginning of a recipe, such as mustard seeds. These need to be 'popped' in hot oil so that the

Opposite: Many Indian spices add colour and texture as well as flavour. From top: Whole dried red chillies, cumin seeds, ground turmeric, dried red chilli flakes.

flavour can be released. Cumin seeds are also often started off in this way. When they start to crackle you would then add your 'wet' ingredients such as garlic, ginger and onions. Ground spices are added after you have added the vegetables – they need to go in last otherwise they will burn and change the colour and flavour of the dish. The spice mixture called garam masala is usually always added right at the end of a recipe – it does not need to be cooked for more than a few minutes but will enhance the flavour of a finished dish.

Away with spice racks!

Spices really stay fresh for only about four weeks, although in hot weather some lose their flavour more quickly. Ground spices deteriorate even more quickly than whole ones because their essential oils evaporate more quickly. It is always better, if you can, to buy whole spices and then dry-roast and grind them, as and when you need them. In some cases you can see when ground spices have turned stale – turmeric changes from bright to dull yellow, while chilli powder loses its bright red colour. One of the problems is that people don't realise that their wonderfully decorative spice racks are no good for storing spices, which begin to deteriorate as soon as they're exposed to light. The best way to store them is in airtight tins in a cupboard away from direct sunlight. Because I cook for my family every day, I grind up my spices in small quantities on a regular basis. I like to keep my spices in a spice box – in fact I have two – one is for everyday flavours such as coriander, cumin, turmeric, mustard seeds and fenugreek, while the other is for aromatic spices includng mace, nutmeg, cinnamon and green cardamom. Some spices, such as saffron and asafoetida should always be kept separate as they are quite powerful. My advice is always to buy small quantities at a time. I also often leave my spices quite coarsely ground – the finer they're ground the more quickly they lose their flavour.

My basic garam masala

Every household in India probably has its own special recipe for garam masala, handed down through the generations. In India, the basic mixture also varies from region to region. The spices in this mixture were traditionally those that heated the body and usually include cardamom, cloves, cinnamon and nutmeg. Here is my recipe for garam masala, plus some regional variations. This quantity lasts me for about a month – you may prefer to make less if you are not cooking Indian food on a daily basis.

150 g (5 oz) cumin seeds
60 g (2^1/$_2$ oz) coriander seeds
50 g (2 oz) green cardamom pods
35 g (1^1/$_2$ oz) black cardamom pods
20 x 2.5 cm (1 in) pieces of cinnamon stick
20 g (^{3}/$_4$ oz) cloves
100 g (4 oz) fennel seeds
15 g (^{1}/$_2$ oz) bay leaves
2 whole nutmegs

Dry-roast all the spices by putting them in a hot cast-iron frying pan. Stir over a medium heat for 3 minutes or until the mixture starts smoking slightly. Remove from the heat and allow to cool on kitchen paper. Transfer to a coffee or spice grinder and process until you have a fine powder (although I prefer to leave my mixture quite coarse). Store in a dry airtight container with a tight-fitting lid and keep out of direct sunlight. Use within one month.

South Indian garam masala

8 dried red chillies
1^1/$_2$ teaspoons fenugreek seeds
35 g (1^1/$_2$ oz) coriander seeds
3 teaspoons cumin seeds
1 teaspoon black mustard seeds
15 curry leaves
1^1/$_2$ teaspoons black peppercorns
2–3 green cardamom pods
1 teaspoon ground ginger
1 tablespoon ground turmeric

Dry-roast and grind all the whole spices. Add the ground ginger and turmeric, cool and store in an airtight container.

Preparing garam masala

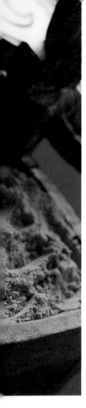

Left: **A spice box containing fenugreek seeds, dried red chilli, mustard seeds, ground turmeric and cumin seeds.**

East Indian garam masala
2 tablespoons fennel seeds
2 tablespoons cumin seeds
3 tablespoons black mustard seeds
1 tablespoon fenugreek seeds
1 tablespoon coriander seeds
3–4 cloves
2.5 cm (1 in) piece of cinnamon stick
2–3 dried red chillies
pinch of asafoetida

Dry-roast and grind all the whole spices. Add the asafoetida and blend together briefly. Cool and store in an airtight container.

North Indian garam masala
8 cm (3 in) piece of cinnamon stick
2 tablespoons cumin seeds
1 tablespoon coriander seeds
4 bay leaves
3–4 black cardamom pods
10 cloves
1 teaspoon black peppercorns
$1/2$ teaspoon ground mace
pinch of ground nutmeg
8 saffron strands

Dry-roast all the whole spices except the saffron. Add the saffron strands, mace and nutmeg, cool and store in an airtight container.

West Indian garam masala
3 tablespoons cumin seeds
4 dried red chillies
2 tablespoons sesame seeds
1 tablespoon fennel seeds
6 green cardamom pods
1 tablespoons ajowan seeds
1 tablespoon coriander seeds
pinch of asafoetida

Dry-roast the whole spices and grind. Add the asafoetida, cool and store in an airtight container.

My kitchen equipment

Indian cooking does not involve complicated cooking techniques so you won't have to buy a lot of specialist equipment. However, these are some of the things I have to hand in my kitchen:

Karhai Also known as a kadai, this is the Indian version of the wok. Made of cast-iron, it is very versatile – you can use it for deep-frying, stir-frying and steaming or for simmering meat. It is ideal to have a ring on top of the burner so that the pan sits steady on it and there is no danger of it tumbling over.

Pans and frying pans Heavy-based pans are ideal as you will be able to cook over a medium heat for longer periods without burning. Tight-fitting lids are also helpful as they stop steam from escaping. A good frying pan, preferably cast-iron, is particularly useful for dry-frying spices before grinding because this type of pan can be heated without any liquid.

Thali Traditionally, this is a large, stainless-steel plate used to serve a whole Indian meal on one plate (see page 93). The food, comprising several different dishes is served in small dishes (katoris). These can be lined around the edge of the plate, while in the centre there will be breads and rice, pickles and poppadums.

Pestle and mortar I use a pestle and mortar for small quantities of whole spices, as well as for crushing garlic and ginger.

Grater A stainless-steel grater can come in handy to grate ginger, garlic, carrot, nutmeg, etc. An Indian grater is used horizontally over a bowl.

Coconut grater I love this piece of equipment – it makes preparing fresh coconut incredibly simple. It clamps to the worksurface and is very useful if you use a lot of freshly grated coconut in cooking. Mine is plastic but traditionally they were metal. You can use an ordinary grater (see page 111).

Tawa This is the traditional flat griddle used to make Indian breads such as chapattis and parathas. Large, flat tawas are sometimes also used to make dosas (flat rice pancakes). Any flat griddle pan can be used as an alternative.

Blender and spice grinder In India I watched spices being ground on an Indian grinding stone, but I find it much easier to use an electric blender for puréeing or blending drinks, soups and sauces. A small spice grinder or coffee grinder is excellent for grinding dry spices.

Knives Since Indian cooking involves a lot of chopping, use good knives with firm handles and sharp steel blades. An all-purpose, medium-sized cook's knife is essential. Sharpen your knives regularly with a steel sharpener.

Tongs A pair of long tongs are useful for turning chapattis on a hot griddle and can also be used for frying pappadums in oil and removing them for draining after.

Skewers When barbecuing meat, fish or vegetables, thick metal skewers are useful as the food does not rotate on the skewer during cooking. Metal skewers do not burn when suspended over live coal and they can also be cleaned and re-used.

Rolling pin/chapatti board Traditional Indian rolling pins are longer and thinner than western ones; we use them to roll out flat breads on a special round chapatti board. However, a conventional rolling pin can also be used to roll out your chapattis on a clean, dry, well-floured work surface.

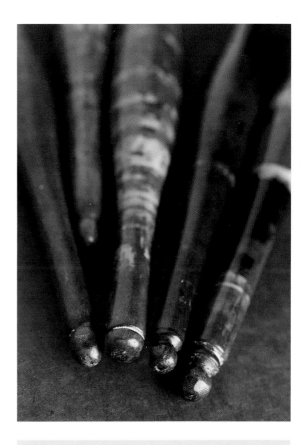

NOTES
- All recipes serve 4 unless otherwise stated.
- Follow either metric or imperial measurements but do not use a mixture of both as they are not interchangeable.

1 teaspoon = 5 ml
1 tablespoon = 15 ml

Flavours of India

Starters, snacks and soups

Indians love to snack. Whatever the time of day you will find little food stalls luring passers-by with all manner of street food. Eating on the hoof is second nature in India and many Indian people just can't resist the temptations of the food stalls, which serve hot, freshly made samosas, pooris and bhajias, to name a few. The snacks in this chapter are sold as street food but they would still be made in the home as well and many of them I learnt at a very young age by watching my grandmother. As entertaining in the home is a very important part of Indian culture, we would often prepare snack items to offer guests who dropped by – who would almost certainly take up the offer. Soups are really only drunk in the north of India and it is only recently that they have begun to be served as a course. They were more usually drunk instead of tea – often in colder climates where you would do what you could to keep warm – and what better way to lift your spirits than to cup your hands around a warming bowl of soup!

Above: **Fast food vendors in the Koyambedu wholesale fruit and vegetable market in Chennai.** *Opposite:* **A roadside stall in Kerala serves spicy chickpeas with spinach to hungry passers-by.**

Samosas

Spicy potato and green pea filled pastries

These tasty snacks are served all over India, from Bombay to Rajasthan. The fillings vary enormously from region to region. In the south, where the population is more Muslim, beef or lamb fillings can be found. For Diwali, samosas are made with sweet fillings. The further north you go, the more pyramid-shaped the samosas tend to become.

Makes 16

250 g (9 oz) potatoes, peeled and cut into chunks
100 g (4 oz) peas, thawed if frozen
3 tablespoons oil or ghee
1½ teaspoons coriander seeds, crushed
15 g (½ oz) fresh root ginger, chopped
5 cloves garlic, chopped
1 green chilli, chopped
2 teaspoons ground coriander
¾ teaspoon ground cumin
½ teaspoon ground fennel
pinch of salt
4 tablespoons fresh coriander, chopped
16 sheets filo pastry, each 8 x 20 cm (3 x 8 in)
** (see My tip)**
flour and water for sealing
vegetable oil for deep-frying

Bring a large pan of salted water to the boil, add the potatoes to the pan and cook for 15–20 minutes until soft. Drain and allow to cool.

Cook the peas in boiling water for 5 minutes, drain and set aside. Roughly mash the potatoes and mix with the peas.

Heat the oil or ghee in a large pan and add the crushed coriander seeds. When they begin to crackle, add the ginger, garlic and green chilli. Fry for 2 minutes. Add the ground spices, sprinkle with water and fry for 3–4 minutes on a low heat. Pour the mixture over the potatoes and peas and mix well. Add the salt and chopped fresh coriander.

Take one rectangle of filo pastry. Place a teaspoon of filling on the top corner. Make the first diagonal fold, then the second and the third (see opposite).

Open up the pouch and spoon in a little more filling, ensuring not to overfill or it will burst whilst being fried. Make a paste with flour and water and smear on the remaining flap. Close and press to 'glue' the opening and seal the filling in the samosa.

Deep-fry a few samosas at a time in hot oil at 190°C (375°F) for 5–10 minutes. Remove from the oil with a slotted spoon and leave to drain on absorbent kitchen paper. Serve warm with Coriander and mint raita or Tamarind and date chutney (see page 111).

◇ **My tip** I use filo pastry as it's easier to use and, because it's lighter, doesn't soak up so much oil. Keep the filo pastry sheets covered with a damp cloth while you are working to prevent them drying out.

Preparing samosas

◈ **My tip** If you have any scraps of filo pastry left over, you can cut them into small pieces and deep-fry in hot oil. They are delicious served with Nimboo ka phool, a zesty, dry dip made from salt, chilli powder, black pepper, sugar and a pinch of citric acid powder.

Khaman dhokla

Steamed chickpea flour pancakes

These pancakes from Gujarat are served as part of a main meal and would most usually be eaten at weekends for brunch. They are quite filling but absolutely delicious.

Serves 4
250 g (9 oz) chickpea flour
100 g (4 oz) natural yogurt
1/2 teaspoon bicarbonate of soda
1/2 teaspoon ground turmeric
1 green chilli, chopped
2.5 cm (1 in) fresh root ginger, chopped
salt, to taste
juice of 1/2 lemon
2 tablespoons vegetable oil
1/2 teaspoon mustard seeds
2 tablespoons chopped fresh coriander
25 g (1 oz) fresh coconut, grated

Mix the chickpea flour with the yogurt and enough warm water to form a thick batter. Mix in the bicarbonate of soda and ground turmeric and allow to ferment for about 1 hour in a warm place.

Using a pestle and mortar crush the green chilli and ginger to a fine paste and add to the chickpea flour and yogurt mixture. Add the salt and lemon juice and mix well.

Grease a shallow cake tin. Pour the batter into the mould and cook in a moderate oven (190°C/375°F/gas 5) for 10–15 minutes. The mixture will have risen to about 4 cm (1½ in). Allow to cool and cut into 4 cm (1½ in) squares. Arrange on a serving dish.

Heat the oil in a small pan and add the mustard seeds. When they begin to crackle pour over the cooked dhoklas.

Serve garnished with chopped coriander and grated coconut.

Pakoras

Vegetable fritters

These are a favourite snack all over India. Chickpea flour is most commonly used for the batter and really gives the best crispness, although you could use plain flour or a mixture of plain flour and rice flour.

Serves 4
200 g (7 oz) chickpea flour
1/2 teaspoon ground turmeric
pinch of asafoetida
salt, to taste
vegetable oil for deep-frying
2 onions, peeled and cut into 2.5 cm (1 in) dice
2 red peppers, cut into 2.5 cm (1 in) dice
2 green peppers, cut into 2.5 cm (1 in) dice
12 spinach leaves, washed
2 potatoes, peeled and cut into thin slices

Mix together the chickpea flour, ground turmeric, asafoetida and salt. Add 300 ml (10 fl oz) water, a little at a time, and mix to make a thick smooth batter.

Heat the oil in a deep-fryer or large, heavy-based saucepan to 190°C (375°F). Dip each piece of vegetable into the batter to coat completely.

Fry in the hot oil, one or two at a time, until they turn golden brown, about 5 minutes. Remove from the oil with a slotted spoon and drain on kitchen paper.

Serve immediately with tomato ketchup or Coriander and mint raita (see page 110).

Opposite: **Vegetable fritters**

Pyaaz ke bhajie

Onion bhajias

These delicious, light, crisp snacks are immensely
popular all over India and are a far cry from
the heavy, stodgy versions found in many
Indian restaurants. If I ever have any left over
(and this would be a rarity in my family), I love
them roughly chopped and added to a fresh
crunchy salad.

Serves 4–6
300 g (11 oz) chickpea flour
1 teaspoon garlic pulp
1/2 teaspoon ground turmeric
3/4 teaspoon red chilli powder
salt, to taste
1/4 teaspoon asafoetida
400 g (14 oz) onions, sliced
2 tablespoons chopped fresh coriander
oil for deep-frying

Mix together the chickpea flour, 50–75 ml
(2–3 fl oz) water, garlic, ground turmeric, red chilli
powder, salt and asafoetida to form a thick paste.
   Add the sliced onions and chopped coriander.
Make small dumplings and deep-fry in batches in
hot oil for 10–15 minutes until they turn golden
brown and the dumplings are cooked through.
Remove with a slotted spoon and drain on
absorbent kitchen paper.

Batata vada

Spiced potato dumplings

Batata vada is traditionally street food, although it can also be served as an accompaniment to a main meal. This is a very simple recipe and is a real favourite all over India. I've used ghee here for an extra buttery flavour.

Serves 4

3 large potatoes, peeled, boiled and mashed
¾ teaspoon salt
¼ teaspoon coarsely ground black pepper
2 green chillies, finely chopped
50 g (2 oz) water chestnut flour or cornflour
1 tablespoon chopped fresh coriander
1 teaspoon lemon juice
4 tablespoons ghee for shallow-frying

Place all the ingredients except the ghee together in a large bowl and mix well. Knead and make into small balls and then flatten into discs.

Heat the ghee in a shallow frying pan. Fry the potato discs on both sides for about 2–4 minutes or until they turn crisp and golden. Drain on kitchen paper and serve hot or cold with a dip or raita.

◇ **My tip** If you can't get hold of water chestnut flour soak 2 slices of bread in ¼ cup of water. Mash, press the excess moisture out and add to the remainder of the ingredients. You might have to tweak the spicing up in order to obtain the desired flavour.

Khandvi

Chickpea flour pancake rolls

This is a Gujarati dish that I would normally serve as part of a main meal. Ideal dishes to go with it are Princess salad (see page 109), Cauliflower with fresh coriander and tomato (see page 85), and of course breads and samosas.

Serves 4

2.5 cm (1 in) fresh root ginger, chopped
1 green chilli, chopped
100 g (4 oz) natural yogurt
½ teaspoon ground turmeric
salt, to taste
150 g (5 oz) chickpea flour, sieved
juice of ½ lemon
4 tablespoons vegetable oil
½ teaspoon mustard seeds
pinch of asafoetida
25 g (1 oz) fresh coconut, grated
2 tablespoons chopped fresh coriander

Crush the ginger and green chillies to a fine a paste using a pestle and mortar.

Grease a large metal baking sheet.

In a large pan, mix together the yogurt, 100 ml (3½ fl oz) water, turmeric, salt and ginger and green chilli paste. Stir in the chickpea flour and lemon juice, ensuring that there are no lumps.

Place the pan over a moderate heat, stirring constantly to form a thick batter.

Quickly spread the mixture over the greased metal surface as thinly as possible whilst the batter is still hot.

Allow to cool down for 2–3 minutes then roll up from one edge to the other to form a layered cylindrical shape. Cut into 2.5 cm (1 in) pieces and place on a serving dish.

Heat the oil and add the mustard seeds. When they begin to crackle add the asafoetida and pour over the pieces. Serve garnished with grated coconut and chopped coriander.

Poricha yera

Spiced fried prawns

This is quite spicy but is wonderful as a starter.
If you wish to serve it as a main dish, the
quantities shown here will serve 2–3 people,
I would serve it with yogurt or raita, bread
and greens.

Serves 4–6
1 kg (2 lb) large raw prawns, cleaned, peeled and
    de-veined with tails left on
salt, to taste
1 tablespoon lemon juice
1 teaspoon garlic pulp
3/4 teaspoon ground turmeric
2 1/2 teaspoons chilli powder
1/2 teaspoon ground fennel
2 1/2 teaspoons ground cumin
1 egg yolk
vegetable oil for deep-frying
lemon wedges, to garnish

Sprinkle the prawns with a pinch of salt and a
teaspoon of lemon juice and set aside.

Mix together the remaining lemon juice, garlic
pulp, turmeric, chilli powder, ground fennel,
ground cumin, egg yolk and salt. Marinate the
prawns in the mixture and leave for 20 minutes.

Deep-fry the prawns in the oil for about 5–10
minutes until cooked, then serve hot with lemon
wedges to garnish.

Ajwaini jheenga

Ajowan prawns

This dish comes from Hyderabad where ajowan
seeds are used a lot with fish. I would serve this
with a paratha or rice, vegetables and a raita.

Serves 4
1 lemon
450 g (1 lb) large raw prawns, cleaned, peeled
    and de-veined
250 g (9 oz) natural yogurt
4 teaspoons garlic pulp
1/2 teaspoon ground turmeric
1 teaspoon garam masala
2 teaspoons ajowan seeds
salt, to taste
2 tablespoons oil
1 tablespoon chopped fresh coriander

Squeeze the juice of half the lemon over the
prawns. Mix well and set aside. Mix the yogurt
with all the remaining ingredients except the oil
and coriander. Add the prawns to the marinade
and refrigerate for 2–3 hours.

Skewer the prawns and cook over charcoal or
under a grill on a greased tray for a few minutes,
turning once. Serve hot with the remaining
lemon squeezed over and garnished with
chopped coriander.

Opposite: **Spiced fried prawns**

Jheenga achaari salaat

Chilli prawn salad

On my travels throughout India, I am always fascinated by the variety of ingredients used for salads. This is a spicy salad from southeast Bengal, which is served cold. If there is any left over, it is absolutely delicious on toast or you can try serving it in vol-au-vent cases as a canapé.

Serves 4

2 tablespoons vegetable oil
300 g (11 oz) large raw prawns, cleaned, peeled and de-veined with tails left on
1 tablespoon tomato purée
150 g (5 oz) onions, chopped
150 g (5 oz) green peppers, chopped
1 tablespoon lemon juice
2 tomatoes, chopped
1 green chilli, chopped
2 tablespoons chopped fresh coriander
2 tablespoons mango pickle
3 tablespoons mustard oil (see My tip)
salt, to taste
1 teaspoon sugar
chopped fresh coriander, to garnish

Heat the vegetable oil in a large frying pan or karhai, add the prawns and stir-fry for 3–4 minutes over a medium heat.

Stir in the tomato purée then remove from the heat and put into a bowl large enough for the other ingredients to be mixed in later. Allow to cool for 30–45 minutes.

Mix in the remaining ingredients and serve cold, sprinkled with chopped coriander.

◇ **My tip** Mustard oil is often used in Indian cooking – it has a rich, nutty flavour that I love.
I also like to use the oil from a jar of mango pickle – it is wonderful for adding flavour as all the spice flavours from the pickle will have been absorbed by the oil.

Tandoori macchi

Fish kebabs

These delicious fish kebabs are best cooked over charcoal, although you can cook them under a grill or on a gas barbecue. The ajowan seeds have excellent digestive properties and are used extensively in barbecue fish recipes. Serve with bread and raita, a vegetable dish or a dal.

Serves 4

juice of ¹/₂ lime
400 g (14 oz) cod or haddock, cut into 5 cm (2 in)
**   cubes**
chopped fresh coriander, to garnish

For the marinade:

250 g (9 oz) thick natural yogurt
1 tablespoon garlic pulp
2 teaspoons ginger pulp
1 tablespoon salt
1 teaspoon garam masala
1 teaspoon ajowan seeds
1 tablespoon vegetable oil

Make the marinade by mixing together the yogurt, garlic, ginger, salt and garam masala in a bowl. Sprinkle the ajowan seeds over and pour the oil over the surface of the yogurt mixture.

Squeeze the lime juice over the pieces of fish and then immerse them in the yogurt marinade. Place in the refrigerator for at least 2 hours.

When you are ready to barbecue, thread the pieces of fish on to skewers.

Cook suspended over the heat for about 15 minutes. Make sure that the pieces of fish do not touch any of the coals or the wire mesh. Turn frequently and baste with a little oil.

Serve garnished with chopped coriander.

Hariyali tikka

Green chicken kebabs

Hariyali means 'green' and this dish gets its name from the spinach and lovely fresh green herbs used in the marinade. It is great as a starter but could also be served as a main course with a dal, rice and some bread. A similar dish is made in the southern states of Hyderabad. I love this served with Lentils with cream and butter (see page 106) or a buttery paratha (see page 99).

Serves 4

150 g (5 oz) spinach leaves
25 g (1 oz) fresh mint
25 g (1 oz) fresh coriander
1 green chilli
200 g (7 oz) natural yogurt
1 tablespoon garlic pulp
1 egg yolk
1 teaspoon garam masala
salt, to taste
450 g (1 lb) chicken breast, skinned and cut into
**   2.5–4 cm (1–1¹/₂ in) cubes**

Bring a large pan of salted water to the boil and blanch the spinach leaves quickly. Drain and refresh by plunging in cold water. Drain again and place in a food processor or blender with the mint, coriander and green chilli. Process to a fine paste and set aside.

Mix the yogurt with the garlic pulp, egg yolk, garam masala and the green paste. Mix well and add the salt. Add the chicken pieces, cover and set aside for 4–5 hours.

The chicken can either be skewered and cooked over charcoal or arranged on a greased tray and cooked under a grill or inside the oven. These kebabs will take about 10 minutes to cook.

Opposite: **Fish kebabs and Green chicken kebabs**

Elaichi malai tikka

Cardamom-flavoured chicken

This delicately scented dish comes from the Muslim state of Hyderabad, where almonds and nuts are used a lot in the cooking. Elaichi means 'cardamom', malai means 'cream' and tikka refers to the fact that the chicken is in bite-size pieces.

Serves 4

500 g (1¹/₄ lb) chicken breast, skinned and cut into
   2.5–4 cm (1–1¹/₂ in) cubes
juice of 1 lemon
250 g (9 oz) natural yogurt
2 tablespoons garlic pulp
1 teaspoon ground cardamom
50 ml (2 fl oz) single cream
1 egg yolk
25 g (1 oz) ground almonds
salt, to taste
¹/₂ teaspoon garam masala
2 tablespoons chopped fresh coriander
oil for greasing
thinly sliced onions and chopped fresh coriander,
   to garnish

Wash and pat dry the chicken and then squeeze over the lemon juice. Rub into the chicken and set aside.

Mix the yogurt with all the remaining ingredients except the oil and whisk well. Add the chicken pieces and set aside to marinate for about 5–6 hours.

The chicken can be either skewered and cooked over charcoal or arranged on a greased tray and cooked under a grill or inside the oven. Cook for about 10–15 minutes.

Serve with an accompaniment of fresh onion rings and chopped fresh coriander to garnish.

Seekh kebab

Minced lamb kebab

There are lots of versions of this dish but this is the one I make at home for my family. The papaya tenderises the meat. Ground coriander can be used instead of turmeric or you can leave out the garlic and add more ginger. A good way of serving these kebabs is in a chapatti wrap with a yogurt raita and fresh coriander, accompanied by thinly sliced onions and a tomato salad.

Serves 4

450 g (1 lb) minced lamb
100 g (4 oz) onions, sliced
1 tablespoon garlic pulp
4 teaspoons ginger pulp
3 tablespoons chopped fresh mint
3 tablespoons chopped fresh coriander
3/4 teaspoon red chilli powder
1/2 teaspoon ground turmeric
1 teaspoon garam masala
25 g (1 oz) fresh papaya
salt, to taste
50 g (2 oz) butter, melted

Mix all the ingredients together except the butter. Place in a food processor or blender and process until you have a coarse paste. Mix in half the melted butter.

Take a handful of the mixture and wrap it around a skewer to form a sausage shape about 10 cm (4 in) long and 2.5 cm (1 in) in diameter. Roll in the hands to ensure the meat is firmly compressed around the skewer. Repeat with the remaining mixture to make 8 kebabs.

Cook over charcoal or under a hot grill for about 10 minutes. Remove from the skewer and smear with the remaining melted butter or oil and serve hot.

◇ **Note** The kebabs can be cooked under the grill or on a gas barbecue but the traditional flavour from the charcoal will be lost.

Left: **Minced lamb kebab**

Gajjar ka shorbha

Carrot and coriander soup

Carrot and coriander soup has become something of a classic – the pungent, slightly citrus flavour of coriander complements the sweet flavour of carrots perfectly. This Indian version is spicier and has more of a kick.

Serves 4

250 g (9 oz) carrots, roughly chopped
100 g (4 oz) onions, sliced
1 tablespoon ginger pulp
1 tablespoon garlic pulp
1 litre (1³/4 pints) water
2 teaspoons ground coriander
³/4 teaspoon red chilli powder
¹/2 teaspoon ground turmeric
1 teaspoon ground fennel
¹/2 teaspoon ground cumin
150 g (5 oz) tomatoes, chopped
2 tablespoons vegetable oil
20 g (³/4 oz) chickpea flour
1 teaspoon sugar
juice of ¹/2 lemon
25 g (1 oz) fresh coriander, chopped
salt, to taste

Place the carrots in a pan with the sliced onions, ginger, garlic and water. Add all the ground spices, stir together and bring to the boil. Lower the heat and simmer for about 1 hour or until the carrots become very soft.

Remove from the heat and add the tomatoes. Allow to cool and then process in a food processor or blender or pass through a sieve. Strain the liquid and set aside.

Heat the oil in another pan and over a moderate heat, add the chickpea flour. Cook for about 2–3 minutes, stirring to make a paste. Pour in the carrot stock, a little at a time, whisking well to avoid any lumps forming until all the stock is used up. Increase the heat and cook for about 5 minutes. Add the sugar, lemon juice and half of the coriander. Season and serve garnished with the chopped coriander.

Mattar aur hare pyaaz ka shorbha

Green pea and spring onion soup

This lovely, fresh soup is best made with fresh shelled peas but if they are not in season, use frozen peas.

Serves 4

2 tablespoons vegetable oil
100 g (4 oz) onions, sliced
1 tablespoon garlic pulp
4 teaspoons ginger pulp
300 g (11 oz) peas, thawed if frozen
¹/2 teaspoon ground turmeric
¹/2 teaspoon ground cumin
1.5 litres (2¹/2 pints) water
2 teaspoons garam masala
2 tablespoons chopped fresh mint
juice of ¹/2 lemon
salt, to taste
15 g (¹/2 oz) cornflour
50 g (2 oz) spring onions, sliced in small rounds
2 tablespoons chopped fresh coriander, to garnish

Heat the oil in a large heavy-based pan and fry the onions, garlic and ginger for 2 minutes. Add the peas and cook, stirring, for about 5 minutes. Add the ground turmeric and cumin.

Add the water, bring to the boil and simmer for about 25 minutes. Remove from the heat, allow to cool and then place the mixture in a food processor or blender. Process to a fine purée and then pass through a strainer. Add the garam masala, chopped mint, lemon juice and salt.

In a small bowl mix the cornflour with a little water until you have a thin liquid the same consistency as cream. Bring the soup to the boil again and thicken with the cornflour mixture, whisking in a little at a time.

Sprinkle the spring onions over the soup with the chopped coriander.

Handmade pappadums

Jehangiri shorbha

Spicy chicken soup

Another warming north Indian dish, this is acutally more of a broth than a soup. If you can't get hold of chicken bones, use 1.5 litres (2¹/₂ pints) of chicken stock instead.

Serves 6–8

2 kg (4¹/₂ lb) raw chicken bones
500 g (1¹/₄ lb) onions, sliced
1 tablespoon garlic pulp
4 teaspoons ginger pulp
³/₄ teaspoon ground turmeric
1 tablespoon ground coriander
1 teaspoon ground fennel
1¹/₂ teaspoons ground cumin
8 cardamom pods
5 bay leaves
8 cloves
400 g (14 oz) can chopped tomatoes
75 g (3 oz) fresh coriander
50 g (2 oz) fresh mint
50 ml (2 fl oz) vegetable oil
75 g (3 oz) chickpea flour
¹/₂ teaspoon salt
juice of ¹/₂ lemon
chopped mint leaves and finely diced poached chicken, to garnish

First make the stock. Place the chicken bones in a large, heavy-based saucepan and cover with cold water. Add all the ingredients except the oil, chickpea flour, salt, lemon juice and mint leaves and bring to the boil. Simmer for 3–4 hours until the water is reduced to one-third of its original quantity. Strain the stock through a fine sieve or muslin cloth and put into another pan to boil.

In a separate pan combine the oil and chickpea flour and cook, stirring, for 2–3 minutes on a low heat. When the chickpea flour begins to bubble add the mixture to the strained chicken stock and bring to the boil, ensuring that no lumps form and the stock becomes slightly thicker in consistency.

Add the salt and lemon juice. Serve garnished with diced chicken and mint.

Left: A pappadum factory in Chennai. Pappadums are one of the most popular snacks in India and are eaten with most main meals. They are made from a split-pea dough, which can be left plain or flavoured with black pepper, chillies or garlic. They are then shaped by hand into small round patties, rolled into thin discs and then left to dry out in the sun.

Fish and shellfish

India's coastline stretches for nearly 7000 kilometres, so it's not surprising that fishing is a major industry. Fresh fish is now available in most of the big cities of India, many of which are miles from the sea, although it holds a particularly special place in the cuisine of the coastal regions.

In southern India coconut palms line the beaches so, for example, Kerala has become famous for its fish curries, delicately scented with coconut. To the north, Bombay and Calcutta all have their own special dishes, depending on what else is grown in the region and what the historical influences have been. The Parsis, who settled on the west coast, like their food sweet and sour, so dishes from Bombay often use a lot of jaggery and tamarind, whereas Bengalis love to flavour fish with a pungent, mustard seed paste. Some of the varieties of fish used in Indian cooking are different from those used in cooler climes but shellfish such as prawns and lobster are very popular. Pomfret is probably my favourite fish. This nicely shaped flat fish is perfect for shallow-frying, grilling, baking, or steaming in banana leaves. It is available from good fishmongers (often in frozen form from overseas) but you can substitute other firm white fish such as monkfish, sea bass or swordfish.

Above: **A basket of fish, fresh out of the sea, and a local fishing boat on the beach at Chennai.** *Opposite:* **Selecting fresh prawns at a seafood stall right by the sea in Cochin.**

Jheenga curry

Goan prawn curry

This is a very simple, easy recipe of which there are many different versions. This is my favourite one – I love to eat this curry with just plain rice.

Serves 4
4 tablespoons vegetable oil
150 g (5 oz) onions, sliced
3 green chillies, sliced
100 ml (3½ fl oz) coconut milk
350 g (12 oz) large peeled raw prawns
15 g (½ oz) tamarind pulp
salt, to taste

For the paste:
200 g (7 oz) desiccated coconut
8 whole dried red chillies
4 teaspoons coriander seeds
2½ teaspoons cumin seeds
½ teaspoon ground turmeric
1 teaspoon ginger pulp
1 teaspoon garlic pulp
2 teaspoons black peppercorns

Place all the ingredients for the paste in a food processor or blender and process until you have a fine paste, adding a little water as necessary.

Heat the oil in a wok or karhai and sauté the onions until golden brown. Add the ground paste mixture and cook, stirring, for 2 minutes.

Add the green chillies and a little water to thin the paste to a sauce consistency. Add the coconut milk and raw prawns and simmer for 5 minutes.

Add the tamarind pulp and salt. Cook for a further 2 minutes and then serve with plain rice.

Karhai jheenga

Prawns in a spicy tomato sauce

This is now eaten more in northern India, although it originated on the east coast. It takes its name from the karhai, the round-bottomed, cast-iron pan in which it is cooked.

Serves 4
2 tablespoons oil
1 teaspoon cumin seeds
200 g (7 oz) onions, diced
1 tablespoon garlic pulp
1 tablespoon ginger pulp
250 g (9 oz) tomatoes, chopped
½ teaspoon ground turmeric
½ teaspoon red chilli powder
400 g (14 oz) large raw prawns, cleaned, peeled
   and de-veined
salt, to taste
pinch of sugar
½ teaspoon crushed black peppercorns
1 teaspoon crushed coriander seeds
1 teaspoon ground fennel
½ teaspoon dried red chilli flakes
3 tablespoons chopped fresh coriander, to garnish

Heat the oil, add the cumin seeds and when they begin to crackle add the diced onions and fry for 10 minutes. Add the garlic and ginger and fry for another minute. Stir in the chopped tomatoes, turmeric and red chilli powder.

Sauté and cook for 10 minutes, stirring constantly. Sprinkle with a little water if needed.

When the oil begins to separate add the prawns, salt to taste and sugar and cook for 8–10 minutes.

Add the crushed black pepper, coriander seeds, ground fennel and crushed red chillies. Cook for a further minute and add half of the chopped coriander.

Sprinkle with the remaining coriander and serve with rice or parathas.

Opposite: **Prawns in a spicy tomato sauce**

Chingri malai curry

Prawns in a coconut cream sauce

This is a dish from the east coast of India. I always use fresh prawns but frozen prawns will also work well.

Serves 4

350 g (12 oz) onions, chopped

4 cloves garlic

1 teaspoon ginger pulp

1 kg (2 lb) large raw prawns, cleaned, peeled and deveined

salt, to taste

3/4 teaspoon ground turmeric

4 tablespoons mustard or vegetable oil

4 cloves

4 green cardamom pods

2.5 cm (1 in) piece of cinnamon stick

2 bay leaves

3/4 teaspoon red chilli powder

50 g (2 oz) natural yogurt

350 ml (12 fl oz) coconut milk

Place the onions, garlic and ginger in a food processor or blender and process to a fine paste.

Smear the prawns with a little salt and half the turmeric. Heat 1 tablespoon of the oil in a frying pan or karhai and fry the prawns over a high heat until just golden brown. Remove and set aside.

Add the remaining oil to the pan and add the cloves, cardamom, cinnamon and bay leaves. Reduce the heat, and add the onion, garlic and ginger paste to the pan. Stir-fry over a medium heat for 2 minutes.

Add the remaining turmeric and red chilli powder. Sprinkle with a little water and stir well. Add the yogurt and mix well. Pour in the coconut milk and return the prawns to the pan. Cook over a medium heat for 5–8 minutes until the prawns are cooked and the sauce thickens.

Serve with plain boiled rice.

Jheenga patio

Prawns with coconut and cashew nuts

Patio is a very typical Parsi dish from the west coast of India. The Parsis settled here after fleeing from Iran in the seventh century. Their food is typically sweet and sour, which is why ingredients such as jaggery and tamarind feature in their dishes.

Serves 4

100 g (4 oz) unsalted cashew nuts

100 g (4 oz) poppy seeds

200 g (7 oz) grated coconut

25 g (1 oz) tamarind pulp

4 tablespoons oil

3 teaspoons garlic pulp

1 teaspoon cumin seeds

10–12 curry leaves

1/2 teaspoon ground turmeric

1 teaspoon red chilli powder

25 g (1 oz) jaggery or brown sugar

salt, to taste

400 g (14 oz) large raw prawns, cleaned, deveined

Soak the cashew nuts and poppy seeds in water for a few hours and then drain. Grind to a fine paste using a pestle and mortar with the grated coconut and tamarind pulp, adding a little water if needed. Set aside.

Heat the oil in a karhai, wok or large frying pan, add the garlic pulp and stir-fry for a few minutes until brown. Add the cumin seeds and curry leaves; after a minute add the turmeric, red chilli powder and jaggery. Stir-fry for a couple of minutes.

Add the coconut and cashew nut paste to the pan and stir quickly, adding a little water to make the sauce thinner. Bring to the boil and then add the prawns. Cook, stirring, for about 10 minutes, or until the prawns are cooked.

Serve with a dal, rice, Mixed vegetable raita (see page 111) or Vegetable biryani (see page 84).

Left: **Prawns in a coconut cream sauce**

Poricha meen
Grilled fish fillets

This dish comes from the coastal region on the southernmost tip of India. I generally use pomfret, but you could use other firm-fleshed fish such as thick salmon or swordfish steaks or halibut or cod fillets.

Serves 4

675 g (1½ lb) thick fish steaks (or thick skinless fillets) such as pomfret, halibut, salmon or swordfish

1 teaspoon garlic pulp

1 teaspoon chilli powder

½ teaspoon ground turmeric

salt, to taste

2 tablespoons lemon juice

Pat the fish dry and place on a plate.

Place the garlic, chilli powder, turmeric, salt and lemon juice in a bowl and mix well to combine the flavours. Smear the fish with this mixture and set aside to marinate for 30 minutes.

Preheat a grill to very hot and then lower to medium heat. Grill the fish for approximately 10 minutes on both sides until cooked through.

Serve hot with a bread or a rich rice dish such as Yogurt with rice (see page 96).

Karwari jheenga/machhi

Goan-style fried fish

This dish is popular on the west coast of India, near Goa. Semolina is used to coat the fish to make a light, crisp coating. It can be served as a starter or as part of a main meal.

Serves 4

25 prawns or about 350 g (12 oz) monkfish, cut into
   4 cm (1¹/₂ in) cubes
salt, to taste
1 tablespoon lemon juice
1¹/₂ teaspoons chilli powder
1 teaspoon ground turmeric
1¹/₂ teaspoons garlic pulp
2 teaspoons tamarind pulp
250 g (9 oz) semolina
oil for deep-frying
lemon wedges, to serve

Place the prawns or monkfish in a bowl with the salt and lemon juice and leave to marinate for about 10 minutes.

Add the chilli powder, ground turmeric, garlic pulp and tamarind pulp. Mix to combine the flavours well and set aside for about 45 minutes.

Place the semolina on a shallow plate. Coat each piece of fish with the semolina and dust off the excess.

Deep-fry in batches in medium hot oil until golden brown, about 10 minutes. Remove from the oil with a slotted spoon and drain on absorbent kitchen paper. Serve with lemon wedges.

◇ **My tip** I sometimes use fine breadcrumbs instead of semolina to coat the fish.

Macchi pattice

Spicy fish cakes

These spicy fishcakes are a favourite of mine and are a speciality of Bombay, where I grew up.

Serves 4

50 g (2 oz) butter
50 g (2 oz) chopped onion
¹/₂ teaspoon ground turmeric
2 teaspoons ground coriander
³/₄ teaspoon red chilli powder
freshly ground black pepper
250 g (9 oz) cooked white fish fillet, such as halibut,
   haddock or sea bass
250 g (9 oz) cooked basmati rice
3 eggs
salt, to taste
3 tablespoons chopped fresh coriander
200 g (7 oz) fresh breadcrumbs
flour for dusting
oil for deep-frying

Melt the butter in a frying pan and add the onion, turmeric, coriander, red chilli powder and black pepper. Fry gently for about 5 minutes over a low heat. Set aside to cool.

Place the fish and rice in a food processor or blender and process to a thick paste. Transfer to a large mixing bowl, add the onion and spice mixture, 1 beaten egg, salt and fresh coriander and mix well. Divide into 4 equal portions and shape into patties.

Beat the remaining eggs in a shallow dish and place the breadcrumbs and flour on separate sheets of greaseproof paper. Dust the fishcakes with flour, then dip into the egg and coat with breadcrumbs, pressing the crumbs on lightly.

Heat the oil in a karhai, wok or deep frying pan and fry the fishcakes in batches for about 5 minutes on each side or until they are golden. Drain well and serve with Coriander and mint raita (see page 110).

Patra ni macchi

Fish steamed inside a leaf

This is another Parsi dish. Steaming fish in banana leaves reflects an East African influence; they are also used in Thai cooking. Aluminium foil works just as well.

Serves 4

300 g (11 oz) coconut, freshly grated

75 g (3 oz) fresh coriander, coarsely chopped

3 tablespoons fresh mint leaves

6 cloves garlic

2 teaspoons cumin seeds

2 tablespoons lemon juice

2 teaspoons sugar

salt, to taste

2 tablespoons oil

8–10 curry leaves

4 banana leaves or squares of aluminium foil, cut into 20 cm (8 in) squares

500 g (1¼ lb) fish fillets, such as halibut, haddock or sea bass

Place the coconut, coriander, mint, garlic and cumin seeds with a little water in a food processor or blender and process to a fine paste. Add the lemon juice, sugar and salt.

Heat the oil in a small frying pan and fry the curry leaves until crisp. Add the leaves and their cooking oil to the coconut paste mixture.

Take a banana leaf or a square of aluminium foil and smother a little of the coconut mixture over it. Place a fillet of fish on top and top with more of the mixture.

Carefully wrap and seal the parcels, ensuring that all the paste is enveloped and nothing can escape. Place on a perforated tray.

Place the perforated tray in a steamer and cook for 15–20 minutes.

Serve with a chicken dish such as Chicken with fenugreek (see page 58), bread, rice and vegetables.

Meen kolumbu

Fish curry

This hot and sweet dish is popular in the south of India. I've added fennel seeds, which are an eastern influence.

Serves 4

5 tablespoons vegetable oil

20 g (¾ oz) coriander seeds

½ teaspoon fenugreek seeds

½ teaspoon fennel seeds

4 red chillies

250 g (9 oz) onions, sliced

25 g (1 oz) tamarind pulp

½ teaspoon mustard seeds

10–12 curry leaves

3 cloves garlic, sliced

½ teaspoon ground turmeric

20 g (¾ oz) jaggery or brown sugar

salt, to taste

500 g (1¼ lb) thick fish steaks (or thick skinless fillets) such as pomfret, halibut, salmon or swordfish

Heat half the oil in a pan and add the coriander seeds, fenugreek seeds, fennel seeds and red chillies. Sauté for 5 minutes until the chillies begin to go dark in colour.

Add the sliced onions and fry, stirring constantly, for about 8 minutes. When the onions are soft, remove the mixture and spread on to a tray to cool. When cool, grind to a very fine paste with the tamarind pulp, adding a little water as necessary. Set aside.

In a karhai or large wide frying pan heat the remaining oil, add the mustard seeds and as soon as they begin to 'pop', add the curry leaves, sliced garlic and turmeric. Add the ground onion paste and stir well. Add water to make a sauce consistency. Add the jaggery and salt.

Bring to the boil. Remove any scum from the surface with a slotted spoon and then add the fish pieces. Cook for approximately 10 minutes until the fish is cooked.

This is often eaten with a chicken dish, such as Black pepper chicken (see page 62).

Chicken, eggs and meat

Due to religious beliefs, many Indians practise vegetarianism, but meat is eaten throughout the country by some sections of the community. Hinduism prohibits the eating of beef as to them the cow is sacred, while pork is forbidden to Muslims. Some sects bend the rules, while others impose further restrictions, for example forbidding food that resembles meat, such as tomatoes and beetroot. Eggs are an excellent source of protein and can be cooked in a number of marvellous ways but some staunch vegetarians spurn even these.

However, India does have a rich tradition of meat dishes, with goat, lamb and chicken being the mainstays. In the north you will find the rich lamb biryanis that were introduced by the Mughals, while Goa is famous for its spicy pork vindaloos. When I was a child I used to travel all over India with my father, and his cook opened up for me a whole new world of exotic meat dishes, many of which I would not normally eat at home. In India, meat is bought in a very different way compared to some other countries – if you are after a chicken you will most likely have to choose one from a basket of live birds. As a rule, in India mutton usually means goat meat but lamb is a good substitute and not as difficult to find in supermarkets.

Above: **Selecting red chillies in the Koyambedu wholesale market in Chennai.**

Tawa murgh

Chicken with fenugreek

This dish gets its name from the tawa, the flattish, two-handled Indian frying pan in which it is cooked, but you can just as easily use a large heavy-based pan. It is very similar to a karhai and this dish is sometimes also called Karhai murgh.

Serves 4

2 tablespoons vegetable oil

1 teaspoon cumin seeds

300 g (11 oz) onions, chopped

2 teaspoons garlic pulp

1 small green chilli, chopped

200 g (7 oz) tomatoes, chopped

1/2 teaspoon ground turmeric

3/4 teaspoon red chilli powder

2.5 cm (1 in) fresh root ginger, chopped

1/2 teaspoon black peppercorns, crushed

1/8 teaspoon fenugreek seeds, coarsely ground

350 g (12 oz) chicken breast, skinned and cut into
    2.5–4 cm (1–11/2 in) cubes

salt, to taste

50 g (2 oz) butter

100 ml (31/2 oz) single cream

pinch dried fenugreek leaves (optional)

3 tablespoons chopped fresh coriander, to garnish

Heat the oil in a tawa, wok or non-stick frying pan and add the cumin seeds, chopped onions, garlic pulp and chopped chilli and fry until the onions are light brown.

Add the chopped tomatoes, ground turmeric and chilli powder and cook for 10–15 minutes until the masala leaves the sides of the tawa and the oil starts to separate.

Stir in the chopped ginger, crushed black peppercorns and ground fenugreek seeds and then add the chicken pieces. Cook for 15–20 minutes over a low heat, stirring occasionally. Season to taste.

Finish with butter, cream and dried fenugreek leaves, if using. Sprinkle over the

Above: **Chicken with fenugreek served with Okra and potatoes, rice and chapattis.**

chopped coriander and serve with a dal, bread, rice, raita and a dry vegetable dish such as Okra and potatoes (see page 88).

Murgh lababdar

Chicken in a creamy tomato and onion sauce

This is a good example of Hyderabadi cuisine and it has also become popular in Delhi and Rajasthan. If you want a slightly milder dish, seed and wash the green chillies before using.

Serves 4–6

2 tablespoons vegetable oil

400 g (14 oz) onions, chopped

25 g (1 oz) fresh root ginger, chopped

2 teaspoons garlic pulp

1 small green chilli, chopped

600 g (1¼ lb) tomatoes, chopped

60 g (3 oz) butter

¾ teaspoon red chilli powder

1 kg (2 lb) chicken breast, skinned and cut into
    2.5–4 cm (1–1½ in) cubes

salt, to taste

300 ml (½ pint) cream

2 teaspoons garam masala

large pinch of dried fenugreek leaves

3 tablespoons chopped fresh coriander

Heat the oil in a large heavy-based pan over a low heat. Add the chopped onions, ginger, garlic and green chilli and sauté for about 10 minutes until the onions are a light golden brown colour.

Add the chopped tomatoes, butter and red chilli powder and cook over a low heat for about 40 minutes, stirring at regular intervals until the butter separates from the gravy.

Add the chicken pieces and continue to cook for about 10–15 minutes or until the chicken is cooked through.

Add the salt and cream and cook for another 10 minutes. Finally, stir in the garam masala and dried fenugreek leaves. Sprinkle with chopped fresh coriander and serve with Handkerchief-thin bread (see page 99), a vegetable rice dish and a paneer dish.

Murgh kolhapuri

Aromatic spiced chicken

This comes from Kolhapur in Maharashtra where the people like their food very spicy and aromatic. The same combination of spices used in this recipe is also used in vegetables dishes.

Serves 4

4 tablespoons vegetable oil

200 g (7 oz) onions, sliced

5 teaspoons coriander seeds

1 tablespoon fennel seeds

1 teaspoon black peppercorns

1 teaspoon ground star anise

1 teaspoon ground cardamom

1 teaspoon ground mace

100 g (4 oz) desiccated coconut

1 tablespoon garlic pulp

350 g (12 oz) chicken breast, skinned and cut into
    2.5–4 cm (1–1½ in) cubes

¾ teaspoon chilli powder

½ teaspoon ground turmeric

1 teaspoon ground coriander

salt, to taste

Heat the oil in a karhai, wok or large frying pan and fry the sliced onions for about 10 minutes or until they turn golden brown.

Add the coriander seeds, fennel seeds, black peppercorns, star anise, cardamom, mace, desiccated coconut and garlic pulp and fry for 3–4 minutes over a low heat until the flavours have intensified.

Remove from the heat and set aside. When the mixture has cooled, place in a food processor or blender and process to a very fine paste. Return to the pan and add more water to make a sauce consistency. Bring to the boil and add the chicken, chilli powder, turmeric, ground coriander and salt. Simmer for 15–20 minutes until the chicken is cooked.

Serve with rice or bread or Vegetable biryani (see page 84).

Dhaniya murgh

Coriander chicken

This aromatic dish comes from the north of
India. It uses coriander in all its forms – the
crushed seeds, ground coriander and the fresh
leaves of the herb.

Serves 4

2 tablespoons ghee or vegetable oil

1 teaspoon cumin seeds

1½ teaspoons coriander seeds, crushed

150 g (5 oz) onions, chopped

1 tablespoon garlic pulp

2.5 cm (1 in) fresh root ginger, cut into
   juliennes

1 green chilli, chopped

3/4 teaspoon ground coriander

400 g (14 oz) chicken breast, skinned and cut into
   2.5–4 cm (1–1½ in) cubes

250 ml (8 fl oz) single cream

1 teaspoon garam masala

3 tablespoons chopped fresh coriander

salt, to taste

Heat the oil in a large, heavy-based pan and add
the cumin seeds and crushed coriander seeds.
When they begin to crackle add the chopped
onions and fry for 8–10 minutes.

Stir in the garlic pulp, ginger juliennes and
green chilli and cook for 2 minutes. Then add
the ground coriander, sprinkle with a little water
and cook, stirring, for another couple of minutes.

Add the chicken pieces and sauté for 5
minutes. Add ½ cup of water, lower the heat
and cook for about 5–10 minutes. Stir in the
cream, garam masala and most of the chopped
fresh coriander.

Season and cook for a further 2–3 minutes.
Remove from the heat and sprinkle with the
remaining coriander. Serve with Lentils with
cream and butter (see page 106) or Cauliflower
with green peas (see page 81).

Murgh malai curry

Coconut chicken curry

The word malai actually means 'cream', even
though there is no cream in this recipe. It earns
the name from its thick coconut sauce which is
wonderfully rich and creamy. I love to eat this
with plain boiled rice and pappadums.

Serves 4–6

2 tablespoons ghee or vegetable oil

3 cloves

3 green cardamom pods

100 g (4 oz) onions, chopped

3 cloves garlic, crushed

15 g (½ oz) ground coriander

½ teaspoon mustard powder

1 tablespoon ground cumin

3/4 teaspoon ground turmeric

3/4 teaspoon chilli powder

1 tablespoon ginger pulp

1 kg (2 lb) chicken breast or thigh, skinned and cut
   into 2.5–4 cm (1–1½ in) cubes

600 ml (1 pint) coconut milk

salt, to taste

juice of ½ lemon

Heat the ghee or oil in a pan and add the whole
cloves and cardamom pods. After a minute add
the chopped onion and garlic and fry for 8–10
minutes until the onions become soft and
translucent.

Add all the powdered spices and ginger pulp
and sprinkle over 100 ml (3½ fl oz) water. Cook
over a low heat for 5 minutes and then add the
chicken pieces. Fry for another 2–3 minutes.

Add the coconut milk and cook over a low
heat for 25–30 minutes until the chicken is
cooked. Season and add the lemon juice.

Serve with Green beans with coconut (see
page 90), plain rice, bread and a fresh chutney.

Opposite: **Coconut chicken curry**

Kozhi kurumelagu
Black pepper chicken

This is very popular in southern India. If you
want extra heat, add more black pepper. It is
a wonderfully aromatic dish because of the
cardamom and fennel.

Serves 4

2^1/$_2$ tablespoons vegetable oil or ghee

2 bay leaves

3 cardamom pods

3 cloves

^{1}/$_2$ teaspoon cumin seeds

200 g (7 oz) shallots, sliced

1 tablespoon garlic pulp

^{3}/$_4$ teaspoon ground fennel

2 teaspoons ground coriander

^{1}/$_2$ teaspoon ground turmeric

^{3}/$_4$ teaspoon red chilli powder

250 g (9 oz) tomatoes, chopped

450 g (1 lb) chicken breast, skinned and cut into
    2.5–4 cm (1–1^1/$_2$ in) cubes

1^1/$_2$ teaspoons black peppercorns, crushed

salt, to taste

Heat the oil or ghee in a karhai, wok or frying
pan and when hot, add the whole spices. After a
minute add the sliced shallots and cook for 5–10
minutes until the shallots colour. Add the garlic
pulp and cook, stirring, for 1 minute.

Add the fennel, coriander, turmeric and red
chilli powder and sprinkle with a little water to
prevent sticking. Cook for a further 2 minutes.
Add the chopped tomatoes and continue to
cook, stirring occasionally, over a moderate heat
for 10–15 minutes. Add more water if required.

Add the chicken pieces and continue to cook
for 15–20 minutes over a low heat. Add the
crushed black pepper and season.

Right: **Chicken with spinach with Rice flavoured with cumin
seeds (see page 97)**

Saagwala murgh

Chicken with spinach

Saag usually means spinach but I sometimes use other leafy vegetables, such as watercress or mustard leaves. This goes beautifully with Rice flavoured with cumin seeds (see page 97).

Serves 4

250 g (9 oz) spinach leaves

2¹/₂ tablespoons ghee or vegetable oil

2 bay leaves

3 cloves

3 cardamom pods

1 teaspoon cumin seeds

150 g (5 oz) onion, chopped

5 cloves garlic, finely chopped

1 green chilli, chopped

¹/₂ teaspoon ground turmeric

2 tomatoes, skinned and diced

400 g (14 oz) chicken breast, skinned and cut into
   2.5–4 cm (1–1¹/₂ in) cubes

50 ml (2 fl oz) single cream

salt, to taste

1 teaspoon garam masala

2 tablespoons chopped fresh coriander

Blanch the spinach leaves in boiling water for 2 minutes, drain and purée in a food processor.

Heat the ghee or oil in a karhai, wok or large frying pan, add the whole spices and when they begin to crackle add the chopped onions and fry for 8–10 minutes until the onions begin to change colour.

Add the chopped garlic and green chilli and continue to fry. Add the turmeric and diced tomatoes and fry for 2 minutes.

Add the chicken pieces and cook for 3 minutes over a moderate heat. Add the puréed spinach and continue to cook over a low heat for 15–20 minutes until the chicken is cooked.

Stir in the cream and season. Sprinkle over the garam masala and chopped coriander and cook for another 2 minutes before serving.

Tariwali murgh

Chicken simmered in a tomato sauce

This is a very popular dish in northern India and is wonderfully aromatic. It takes its Indian name from the way it is cooked.

Serves 4

vegetable oil for deep-frying

350 g (12 oz) onions, sliced

300 g (11 oz) fresh tomatoes, chopped or 200 g
    (7 oz) canned

2½ tablespoons vegetable oil or ghee

1 teaspoon cumin seeds

4 cardamom pods

4 cloves

3 bay leaves

1 tablespoon garlic pulp

½ teaspoon ground turmeric

¾ teaspoon red chilli powder

1 teaspoon ground paprika

450 g (1 lb) chicken breast, skinned and cut into
    2.5–4 cm (1–1½ in) cubes

1 teaspoon ground fennel

1 teaspoon sugar

salt, to taste

1 tablespoon natural yogurt

single cream (optional)

chopped fresh coriander, to garnish

Heat the oil in a large heavy-based pan to 190°C (375°F). Deep-fry the sliced onions until they turn golden, stirring frequently. Remove with a slotted spoon and drain on kitchen paper. Put the fried onions and chopped tomatoes in a food processor or blender and process to a smooth paste. Set aside.

In another pan heat the oil or ghee and add the cumin seeds, cardamom pods, cloves and bay leaves. When they begin to crackle add the garlic pulp, turmeric, red chilli powder and paprika. Sprinkle with a little water and cook, stirring, for 3–5 minutes over a low heat. If the spices start to stick to the bottom of the pan, sprinkle with a little water and keep stirring the pan.

Stir in the tomato and onion paste and cook over a low heat for 5–10 minutes. Add the chicken pieces and cook over a low heat for 15–20 minutes, stirring occasionally. Add a little water if the sauce becomes too thick. Stir in the ground fennel.

When the chicken is cooked, add the sugar, salt and yogurt and remove from the heat. Garnish with a swirl of cream, if using, and sprinkle with the chopped coriander.

Murgh mirch masala

Chicken with peppers

This is a colourful dish from the north of India. A southern version of this recipe would use more crushed black pepper and no cream – you can adapt it to your own taste.

Serves 4–6

2 tablespoons vegetable oil or ghee

1 teaspoon cumin seeds

2 cloves

2 cardamom pods

175 g (6 oz) onions, chopped

2 teaspoons garlic pulp

¾ teaspoon red chilli powder

2 teaspoons ground coriander

½ teaspoon ground turmeric

225 g (8 oz) tomatoes, chopped

400 g (14 oz) chicken breast, skinned and cut into
    2.5–4 cm (1–1½ in) cubes

1 red pepper, sliced

1 yellow pepper, sliced

1 green pepper, sliced

1 green chilli, chopped

1 teaspoon black peppercorns, crushed

50 ml (2 fl oz) single cream

½ teaspoon sugar

2 tablespoons chopped fresh coriander

salt, to taste

Heat the oil or ghee in a karhai, wok or frying pan and when hot, put in the cumin seeds, cloves and cardamom pods. When they begin to crackle add the chopped onions

and cook over a medium heat for 10–12 minutes. Add the garlic pulp and cook, stirring, for 2 minutes.

Stir in the ground spices and chopped tomatoes and cook for 10–15 minutes until the oil begins to separate. If the mixture starts to stick to the pan, sprinkle over a little water.

Above: **Chicken with peppers**

Add the chicken and sliced peppers and cook for a further 10–15 minutes. Stir in the remaining ingredients, leaving some coriander to garnish. Season and cook for another 5–10 minutes.

Serve sprinkled with the remaining coriander.

Anda bhurjee

Indian breakfast tortilla

This is a great brunch dish which can also be part of a main meal. As a child I used to love eating it in bread and butter, like a sandwich. It's a mix of scrambled eggs spicy Spanish omelette, which you can adapt to make hotter. It originated in the north but is now eaten all over India.

Serves 4
6 eggs
25 ml (1 fl oz) milk
salt, to taste
1/2 teaspoon ground black pepper
3 tablespoons oil
100 g (4 oz) onions, chopped
1/4 teaspoon ground turmeric
1 green chilli, chopped
1/2 teaspoon ground cumin
75 g (3 oz) tomatoes, skinned, seeded and
finely diced
1 tablespoon chopped fresh coriander

Break the eggs into a bowl, add the milk, salt and pepper and whisk well.

Put the oil in a non-stick frying pan and place over a moderate heat. When hot add the chopped onions, turmeric, green chilli and cumin. Cook, stirring, for 3–5 minutes Add half the diced tomatoes and cook for 1 minute.

Pour in the egg mixture and cook, stirring vigorously with a wooden spoon to avoid the egg sticking to the pan. Sprinkle with chopped coriander and continue to cook until the eggs are done to your taste. Garnish with the remaining coriander and serve.

Opposite: **Egg curry**

Baida curry

Egg curry

As most Indians are non-meat eaters, eggs are a great way of providing necessary protein. I love this recipe – it is quick to make and perfect with chapattis or parathas for brunch, or with rice for a light supper. You could also serve an onion, coriander, chilli, lemon and salt salad on the side.

Serves 4
6 eggs
2 tablespoons vegetable oil or ghee
1 teaspoon cumin seeds
1/2 teaspoon mustard seeds
2 bay leaves
8–10 curry leaves (optional)
3 cloves
3 cardamom pods
175 g (6 oz) onions, sliced
1 tablespoon garlic pulp
1 tablespoon ginger pulp
1 tablespoon ground coriander
3/4 teaspoon red chilli powder
1/2 teaspoon ground turmeric
250 g (9 oz) chopped tomatoes
1/2 teaspoon garam masala
salt, to taste
2 tablespoons chopped fresh coriander

Hard-boil the eggs, shell, cut into quarters and arrange in the base of a serving dish.

Heat the oil or ghee in a karhai or wok and add the cumin seeds, mustard seeds, bay leaves, curry leaves, if using, cloves and cardamom pods. When they begin to crackle add the sliced onions and fry for 10–12 minutes.

Stir in the garlic, ginger, coriander, red chilli powder and turmeric. Sprinkle with a little water and cook, stirring, for 2 minutes. Add the chopped tomatoes and garam masala and cook over a low heat for 10–15 minutes. If the contents of the pan start to stick, add a little more water. Season. Serve by pouring the sauce over the eggs in the serving dish and sprinkle with the fresh coriander.

Kheema kofta curry

Lamb meatballs in a spicy sauce

This is very much a speciality of the northwest region and was originally introduced by the Mughal emperors. There are many variations but this is my preferred recipe.

Serves 4
For the koftas:
250 g (9 oz) minced lamb
75 g (3 oz) onions, chopped
1 tablespoon garlic pulp
1 tablespoon ginger pulp
3/4 teaspoon chilli powder
1 teaspoon ground coriander
2 tablespoons chopped fresh coriander
1 egg, beaten
salt, to taste

For the sauce:
2 tablespoons tomato purée
75 g (3 oz) natural yogurt
1 tablespoon oil
1 teaspoon cumin seeds
1 bay leaf
1 tablespoon garlic pulp
2 teaspoons ginger pulp
1/2 teaspoon ground turmeric
3/4 teaspoon chilli powder
salt, to taste
3/4 teaspoon garam masala

To make the koftas, place the minced lamb in a food processor or blender and process for about 1 minute. Remove and set aside in a large bowl.

Place the onions, garlic, ginger, chilli powder, ground coriander and half of the chopped fresh coriander in the food processor and blend together for about 1 minute. Combine with the minced lamb. Add the egg, season and set aside for 1 hour.

To make the sauce, whisk together the tomato purée and yogurt. Set aside. Heat the oil in a pan and when hot, add the cumin seeds and

bay leaf. When the seeds begin to crackle add the garlic and ginger. Cook, for 1 minute. Add the turmeric and chilli powder and then the yogurt mixture. Add salt and cook for a further 2 minutes.

Take small balls of mince mixture and shape into small koftas (round ball shapes) using well-greased hands. Return the sauce to a high heat and add the koftas. Cover and cook for about 15 minutes, stirring occasionally.

Serve hot, sprinkled with the garam masala and remaining chopped coriander.

Kheema bhurjee

Minced lamb with peas and mint

This is a wonderfully simple and comforting dish and is great served with rice or chapattis. You can also use minced beef but I prefer lamb. If you can buy a good cut and mince it yourself, you will really notice the difference in taste.

Serves 4
2 tablespoons oil
100 g (4 oz) onions, chopped
1/2 teaspoon cumin seeds
2 bay leaves
1 tablespoon garlic pulp
1 tablespoon ginger pulp
3/4 teaspoon chilli powder
1/2 teaspoon ground turmeric
2 teaspoons ground coriander
75 g (3 oz) peas, thawed if frozen
200 g (7 oz) tomatoes, chopped
350 g (12 oz) minced lamb
1 tablespoon chopped fresh mint
2 tablespoons chopped fresh coriander
1 green chilli, chopped
salt, to taste

Heat the oil in a karhai, wok or large heavy-based pan and add the onions. Cook over a moderate heat for 10–15 minutes or until golden brown, then add the cumin seeds and bay leaves.

In a bowl, combine together the garlic pulp, ginger pulp, chilli powder, ground turmeric, ground coriander, peas and chopped fresh tomatoes and add this mixture to the cooked onions in the pan. Cook, stirring constantly, for about 5 minutes.

Add the minced lamb to the mixture and stir-

Above: **Minced lamb with peas and mint**

fry for 10–15 minutes. Stir in the chopped mint, most of the chopped coriander and the green chilli and mix well. Season.

Stir-fry for another 2–3 minutes and serve garnished with the remaining chopped coriander.

Irachi varthathu

Dry-fried lamb with spices

This dish comes from Kerala on the southernmost tip of India. The spices will make it very hot but beautifully aromatic. I serve this with plain boiled rice and a cooling yogurt relish.

Serves 4–6

4 tablespoons oil
2 dried red chillies
3 cloves
3 green cardamom pods
2 cinnamon sticks
1 teaspoon cumin seeds
1 teaspoon fennel seeds
8–10 black peppercorns
2 bay leaves
25 curry leaves
250 g (9 oz) onions, sliced
6–8 cloves garlic, crushed
2.5 cm (1 in) fresh root ginger, sliced
1 kg (2 lb) boned shoulder of lamb, cut into
  2.5–4 cm (1–1½ in) cubes
1 tablespoon ground coriander
½ teaspoon ground turmeric
¾ teaspoon red chilli powder
salt, to taste
25 g (1 oz) desiccated coconut
fried curry leaves and desiccated coconut, to garnish

Heat the oil in a karhai, wok or large, heavy-based pan and, when hot, add all the whole spices and curry leaves. When they begin to crackle add the sliced onions and cook until golden brown in colour. Add the garlic and ginger and cook, stirring, for another 2 minutes.

Add the diced lamb and cook over a high heat until the lamb colours, about 5–10 minutes. Add the ground spices and cook, stirring frequently, for about 10 minutes. Cover and cook over a low heat for a further 10–15 minutes.

Season and stir in the desiccated coconut. Serve garnished with more coconut and fried curry leaves.

Bhuna gosht

Stir-fried lamb with onions

Mutton really is the best meat for this dish and if you can get hold of some from your butcher, do use it. However, lamb is a perfectly good substitute. This dish gets its name from the method of cooking – bhuna means 'stir-fried'.

Serves 4–6

3 tablespoons oil
1 teaspoon cumin seeds
6 cardamom pods
6 cloves
3 bay leaves
400 g (14 oz) onions, sliced
1 tablespoon garlic pulp
2.5 cm (1 in) fresh root ginger, cut into juliennes
1½ teaspoons red chilli powder
4 teaspoons ground coriander
¾ teaspoon ground turmeric
1 kg (2 lb) mutton or lamb, cut into 2.5–4 cm
  (1–1½ in) cubes
salt, to taste
75 g (3 oz) natural yogurt
2 tablespoons chopped fresh coriander

Heat the oil in a large heavy-based pan and add the cumin seeds, cardamom pods, cloves and bay leaves. When the cumin seeds begin to crackle add the sliced onions and cook over a moderate heat for about 15–20 minutes until the onions are nicely browned.

Stir in the garlic, ginger, red chilli powder, ground coriander and turmeric. Add the mutton or lamb cubes, reduce the heat and cook, stirring constantly, for approximately 30 minutes. Add the salt and yogurt and cook for a further 5 minutes. Stir in half the chopped coriander.

Serve hot, sprinkled with the remaining chopped fresh coriander.

Kalimiri gosht

Lamb in a black pepper sauce

This is really a very spicy dish and a favourite with those who like heat and spice. Black pepper is a great flavour enhancer but in increased quantities will give a real kick to a dish.

Serves 4–6

5 teaspoons coriander seeds

5 teaspoons cumin seeds

2 teaspoons black cumin seeds

1 tablespoon black peppercorns

a few saffron strands

225 g (8 oz) natural yogurt

salt, to taste

1 kg (2 lb) boned shoulder of lamb, cut into
    2.5–4 cm (1–1½ in) cubes

150 g (5 oz) ghee

5 green cardamom pods

1 black cardamom pod

5 cloves

2.5 cm (1 in) piece of cinnamon stick

1 bay leaf

250 g (9 oz) onions, sliced

2.5 cm (1 in) fresh root ginger, chopped

2 green chillies, chopped

200 ml (7 fl oz) single cream

1 teaspoon ground fennel

Using a pestle and mortar, crush together the coriander seeds, cumin seeds, black cumin seeds and black peppercorns. Dissolve the saffron in 2 tablespoons of lukewarm water.

Mix the crushed spices with the yogurt and salt and use it to cover the lamb pieces. Leave to marinate for at least 30 minutes.

Heat the ghee in a karhai, wok or large heavy-based pan, add the cardamom pods, cloves, cinnamon and bay leaf and cook over a medium heat until the spices begin to crackle. Add the onions and cook until they turn golden brown, about 15–20 minutes.

Add the ginger and green chillies to the pan and cook, stirring, for 1 minute. Add the

marinated lamb pieces and stir to combine. Add 750 ml (1¼ pints) of water and bring to the boil. Cover and simmer for 25–30 minutes.

Add the saffron liquid and cream and bring back to the boil. Adjust the seasoning, sprinkle with the ground fennel and serve hot.

Gosht biryani

Layered lamb biryani

Biryani is the lasting legacy of the Mughals who once ruled India. These fragrant rice and meat dishes can be eaten as a complete meal. This version would be served for a special occasion, although it is surprisingly easy to make.

Serves 4–6

250 g (9 oz) basmati rice

5 tablespoons oil or ghee

4 cloves

4 cardamom pods

a few saffron strands

50 g (2 oz) natural yogurt

salt, to taste

1 tablespoon garlic pulp

1½ teaspoon ginger pulp

½ teaspoon ground turmeric

1 tablespoon ground coriander

1 teaspoon ground fennel

675 g (1½ lb) boneless lamb, cut into
    2.5 cm (1 in) cubes

150 g (5 oz) onions, sliced

200 g (7 oz) can chopped tomatoes

2 tablespoons chopped fresh coriander

2 tablespoons chopped fresh mint

sliced fried onions and chopped fresh coriander,
    to garnish

Wash the rice in several changes of water and set aside. Take two large pans and to each add 1 tablespoon of oil, 2 cloves and 2 cardamom pods but put the saffron strands in only one pan. Divide the washed rice equally between the two pans. Cover the rice in each pan with boiling water and cook over a medium high

heat for 12–15 minutes, or until the rice is cooked. Drain separately and set aside.

Mix together the yogurt, salt, garlic pulp, ginger pulp and ground spices in a large bowl and add the cubes of lamb. Leave to marinate for at least 1 hour.

In another pan heat the remaining oil or ghee and fry the sliced onions for 8–10 minutes or until golden. Add the chopped tomatoes and the marinated lamb and cook, covered, for 30 minutes, stirring occasionally. Add salt, the chopped coriander and mint. Cook over a high heat to reduce down to a thick sauce.

Take a well-greased ovenproof dish or

Above: **Layered lamb biryani**

pudding bowl and layer the bottom first with boiled rice and then with saffron rice. Spread a layer of lamb mixture over this followed by another layer of the two different rice mixes. Repeat until all the lamb is used up, making sure that the top layer is rice. Place the dish in a preheated oven for 5 minutes so that the flavours can blend together.

To serve, you will need to invert the dish carefully over a large plate and then gently remove. Garnish with the browned onions and chopped fresh coriander.

Achaari gosht

Lamb in a pickled spice sauce

This is a popular dish in western India but is eaten in the north as well. The long list of spices means that this is a wonderfully aromatic dish.

Serves 4–6

2 onions

5 cm (2 in) fresh root ginger, chopped

8 cloves garlic, chopped

1 bay leaf

2 black cardamom pods

2 tablespoons coriander seeds

1/4 teaspoon fenugreek seeds

2 cinnamon sticks

5 cloves

1 teaspoon cumin seeds

pinch of onion seeds

1/2 teaspoon mustard seeds

2 black peppercorns

7 green chillies

75 g (3 oz) ghee or oil

1 kg (2 lb) boned shoulder of lamb, cut into
    2.5–4 cm (1–1 1/2 in) cubes

1/4 teaspoon ground turmeric

3/4 teaspoon red chilli powder

75 g (3 oz) natural yogurt

salt, to taste

1 tablespoon chopped fresh coriander

Chop 1 of the onions and put in a food processor or blender with the ginger, garlic and a little water. Process to a smooth paste.

Using a pestle and mortar, crush together the whole spices. Slit the green chillies in half and set aside.

Heat the ghee or oil in a heavy-based pan over a moderate heat. Add the crushed spices and stir-fry for 1 minute. Slice the other onion and add to the pan. Cook, stirring, for 10–15 minutes or until it turns golden brown.

Add the lamb pieces and stir-fry for 4–8 minutes. Stir in the ginger, garlic and onion paste and cook for a further 10 minutes. Add the

ground turmeric, red chilli powder and yogurt, cover and gently simmer for about 20 minutes. Add the green chillies and continue to cook over a low heat for 15–20 minutes or until the lamb is tender. Season to taste.

Serve hot garnished with chopped coriander.

Salli jardaloo boti

Lamb with apricots and fried potato straws

A traditional Parsi dish that would be prepared for weddings and other religious ceremonies. As always, you can reduce the heat, if you like, by seeding the chillies.

Serves 4–6

4 dried red chillies, diced

5 cm (2 in) piece of cinnamon stick

2 1/2 teaspoons cumin seeds

6 cardamom pods

8 cloves

2 teaspoons ginger pulp

2 teaspoons garlic pulp

1 kg (2 lb) boned shoulder of lamb, cut into
    2.5–4 cm (1–1 1/2 in) cubes

10–15 dried apricots, roughly chopped

5 tablespoons vegetable oil

250 g (9 oz) onions, sliced

125 g (4 1/2 oz) tomatoes, chopped

salt, to taste

2 tablespoons white wine vinegar

25 g (1 oz) sugar

For the potato straws (salli):

2 teaspoons salt

1 large potato, peeled

vegetable oil for deep-frying

Using a coffee or spice grinder, blend together the red chillies, cinnamon sticks, cumin seeds, cardamom pods and cloves to a very fine powder. Mix together half the ginger, half the garlic and half the ground spices. Rub the lamb pieces with this mixture and leave to marinate for at least 1 hour.

Place the apricots in a pan with about 500 ml (18 fl oz) water and bring to the boil. Leave to soak in their cooking water for about 30 minutes, or until they become soft and mushy.

Heat the oil in a karhai, wok or large, heavy-based pan and fry the sliced onions over a medium heat for about 15–20 minutes until they turn a rich brown colour. Add the remaining ginger, garlic and ground spices and cook, stirring, for 2 minutes.

Add the lamb and stir-fry for about 5 minutes. Stir in the chopped tomatoes and salt. Add the vinegar, sugar, apricot mixture and a little water, stir and simmer over a low heat for 25 minutes until the lamb is tender.

To make the potato straws, add the salt to about 450 ml (³/₄ pint) water. Cut the peeled potato into very fine strips and put into the water for 5 minutes. Heat the oil in a large pan or wok. Squeeze the potato strips to remove as much water as possible and fry in the oil until golden brown. Remove and drain on kitchen paper.

To serve, heat the lamb gently and garnish with the potato straws.

Below: **Lamb with apricots and fried potato straws**

Bade aur mirch ki curry

Beef chilli curry

Although beef is forbidden to Hindus, the Anglo-Indians in Goa do eat it. Being lovers of hot dishes, they use chillies in every form – this dish has fresh green chillies, chilli powder and a red chilli garnish!

Serves 4

175 g (6 oz) onions, chopped

5 cloves garlic, chopped

1 cm (1/2 in) fresh root ginger, chopped

3/4 teaspoon red chilli powder

1/2 teaspoon ground turmeric

1 teaspoon ground coriander

1 teaspoon ground cumin

350 g (12 oz) stewing beef, cut into 2.5–4 cm (1–1 1/2 in) cubes

salt, to taste

3 tablespoons oil

3 green chillies, slit lengthways

red chillies, to garnish

Place half the onions, the garlic cloves and chopped ginger in a food processor or blender and grind to a fine paste. Add the ground spices to this paste and combine well. Smear the cubed beef with roughly half the paste and sprinkle with salt. Leave to marinate for 10–15 minutes. Set the remaining paste aside.

Heat half the oil in a large, heavy-based pan and add the remaining chopped onions and the beef. Cook, stirring, for about 5 minutes. Remove from the pan with a slotted spoon and set aside. Add the remaining oil to the pan and stir-fry the green chillies with the remaining paste for 5–6 minutes over a medium heat.

Return the beef and onions to the pan with about 1/2 cup of water. Cook over a high heat for 3–4 minutes. Add salt and simmer for a further 10 minutes, stirring occasionally and adding more water if necessary.

When the beef is cooked, serve with plain boiled rice and garnish with fresh red chillies.

Vindaloo

Beef/pork cooked in vinegar and garlic

This is an authentically east Indian dish from Goa and was probably invented by the Portuguese who settled there. Famous for being searingly hot, it is delicious with plain boiled rice.

Serves 4

450 g (1 lb) beef or pork, cut into 2.5–4 cm (1–1 1/2 in) cubes

2 tablespoons vinegar

salt, to taste

2 tablespoons oil

4 cloves garlic, crushed

250 g (9 oz) onions, sliced

125 g (4 1/2 oz) tomatoes, chopped

4 green chillies, slit lengthways

1/2 teaspoon sugar

For the spice paste:

6 dried red chillies

2 teaspoons bright red paprika powder

1/2 teaspoon ground turmeric

1 teaspoon cumin seeds

5 cm (2 in) piece of cinnamon stick

10 cloves

10–12 black peppercorns

5 cardamom pods

10 cloves garlic

4 cm (1 1/2 in) fresh root ginger, chopped

Place the cubed meat in a large bowl, cover with half the vinegar and some salt and place in the refrigerator for 2 hours.

Place all the spice paste ingredients and the remaining vinegar in a food processor or blender and grind to a fine paste. Rub half of the paste over the meat and marinate in the refrigerator for a further 8 10 hours.

Heat the oil in a large, heavy-based pan and add the crushed garlic. When it begins to change colour add the sliced onions and cook until they are golden brown. Add the chopped tomatoes, the remaining spice paste, green chilli

Above: **Beef chilli curry**

and sugar. Cook over a medium heat for 10–15 minutes.

Add the marinated meat and about 250 ml (8 fl oz) water and cook over a medium heat for 20–25 minutes. Add salt to taste. After about

5–10 minutes check if the meat is tender and cooked. The sauce should have the consistency of thick cream.

Vegetable dishes

Indian fruit and vegetable markets are truly inspiring and a trip to the market is an important part of the food culture – when I was a child I marvelled at the colourful stalls and learnt how to select the best produce and bargain with the sellers. The eating habits of Indians vary enormously depending on religion and region but one thing links us all – our love for vegetables. It is almost taken for granted that you are vegetarian but even when you do eat meat you would almost certainly have at least two or three vegetable dishes with it. Vegetables are not really eaten as an accompaniment in the same way as they are in the West. A typical meal for a true vegetarian would be several vegetable dishes that use a range of different ingredients and thereby provide a balanced meal. Spinach leaves and other greens are cooked with paneer. Potatoes are a popular staple throughout India, while cauliflower, okra, cabbage, corn, aubergine and beans are prepared in a thousand different ways. Lesser-known vegetables such as karela and doodhi are also popular, but it would take forever to name every vegetable. Here are some of my favourite vegetable dishes.

Above: **An early morning at the Koyambedu wholesale market in Chennai.** *Above right:* **Some of the more interesting, as well as the familiar, vegetables on offer.** *Opposite:* **A typical market in Kerala.**

Adraki gobi

Cauliflower with ginger

This dish is eaten all over India. It would most likely be served with other dishes as part of a main meal. Cauliflower is a favourite in my family and because my husband is vegetarian, I cook it for him often.

Serves 4
5 cm (2 in) fresh root ginger
1 tablespoon vegetable oil
1/2 teaspoon cumin seeds
100 g (4 oz) onions, chopped
1/2 teaspoon garlic pulp
1 green chilli, finely chopped
1/4 teaspoon ground turmeric
1/4 teaspoon ground coriander
1/2 teaspoon ground ginger
600 g (1 lb 5 oz) cauliflower, cut into florets
salt, to taste
1 teaspoon ground cumin
3 tablespoons chopped fresh coriander
1 teaspoon lemon juice

Make a pulp with half of the ginger and cut the remaining half into julienne strips.

Heat the oil in a large pan and add the cumin seeds. When they begin to crackle add the onions, followed by the garlic pulp and cook over a moderate heat, stirring, for 10–12 minutes.

Add the ginger pulp and green chilli. Cook for 1 minute then add the ground turmeric, ground coriander and ground ginger, followed by a sprinkle of water. Add the cauliflower and salt and cook over a low heat for 10–15 minutes or until the cauliflower is cooked (it should still retain some bite).

Adjust the seasoning and sprinkle with the ground cumin, some of the chopped coriander (leaving some for a garnish) and the lemon juice.

Serve hot, garnished with more chopped coriander and the ginger julienne strips.

Cachumbar

Cucumber, tomato and onion salad

This is a very popular Indian salad from Gujarat, which is served as an accompaniment in most Indian houses. There are many different combinations, but the recipe below is probably the most popular and the one I make at home.

Serves 4
3 green chillies
250 g (9 oz) red onions, peeled and finely chopped
150 g (5 oz) firm red tomatoes, cut into small wedges
100 g (4 oz) cucumber, peeled and diced
2 tablespoons chopped fresh coriander
3 tablespoons lemon juice
1 teaspoon black mustard seeds, coarsely crushed
1 teaspoon sugar
salt, to taste

Chop the green chillies. Seed them first if you want the salad to be less hot.

Combine all the ingredients in a bowl and toss well. Cover and keep at room temperature for at least 15–20 minutes before serving so that the flavours develop.

◇ **My tip** If you have any cachumbar left over, it is delicious added to natural yogurt to make a raita. Add some more chopped coriander and a couple of pinches of red chilli flakes and refrigerate for a couple of hours.

Gobi mutter

Cauliflower with green peas

This beautifully colourful dish comes from northern India and is a typical Gujarati recipe. It is also eaten in East India where they add more garam masala.

Serves 4

3 tablespoons vegetable oil
1 teaspoon cumin seeds
2 teaspoons garlic pulp
1 teaspoon chopped fresh root ginger
1 small green chilli, chopped
1/2 teaspoon ground turmeric
500 g (1 1/4 lb) cauliflower, cut into florets
100 g (4 oz) peas, thawed if frozen
salt, to taste
2 tablespoons chopped fresh coriander
1/2 teaspoon ground cumin
1/2 teaspoon garam masala
juice of 1/2 lemon

Heat the oil in a karhai, wok or large pan and, when hot, add the cumin seeds, followed by the garlic, ginger and green chilli.

Add the ground turmeric, cauliflower, peas and salt. Sprinkle with a little water, stir, cover the pan and cook for 10–15 minutes.

When the cauliflower is cooked, stir in the chopped fresh coriander, ground cumin, garam masala and lemon juice. Mix well and serve immediately.

◇ **My tip** Fresh shelled peas are best for this recipe but you can use frozen peas or even sliced mangetout, snowpeas or French beans.

Left: **Cauliflower with green peas**

Batata nu saak

Spicy potatoes in a tomato sauce

This dish comes from Gujarat, where the local people love sweet, spicy and sour flavourings. Originally, it would not have had the curry leaves and the desiccated coconut. Serve for brunch with pooris or for a main meal with Rice flavoured with cumin seeds (see page 97), natural yogurt and mango pickle.

Serves 4

4 tablespoons vegetable oil

3/4 teaspoon mustard seeds

1 teaspoon cumin seeds

1/2 teaspoon dried red chillies

1/4 teaspoon ground asafoetida

10–12 curry leaves

450 g (1 lb) potatoes, peeled and diced

3/4 teaspoon red chilli powder

1/2 teaspoon ground turmeric

2 teaspoons ginger pulp

1 green chilli, chopped

150 g (5 oz) tomatoes, chopped

1/2 teaspoon ground coriander

20 g (3/4 oz) desiccated coconut

25 g (1 oz) jaggery or brown sugar

salt, to taste

20 g (3/4 oz) tamarind paste

2 tablespoons chopped fresh coriander

Heat the oil in a pan, add the mustard seeds, cumin seeds, dried red chillies and asafoetida. After 1 minute add the curry leaves and stir.

Add the potatoes, red chilli powder, ground turmeric, ginger and green chilli. Stir-fry over a high heat for about 30 seconds. Add 200 ml (7 fl oz) water, cover and simmer for 5 minutes.

Stir in the chopped tomatoes, ground coriander, coconut, jaggery and salt and cook for 10 minutes. Add the tamarind paste and half of the chopped coriander and cook for a further 2 minutes. Sprinkle with the remaining chopped coriander and serve.

Kaikari ishtu

Vegetables in coconut milk

The coconut milk in this dish tells you that it originated in southern India, where it is used extensively in cooking. The vegetables used can vary – here I've used potatoes, cauliflower, carrots and peas. I would eat this dish with plain boiled rice, chapattis or uttapam. It also makes a great accompaniment to a fish curry.

Serves 4

4 tablespoons oil

3/4 teaspoon mustard seeds

10–12 curry leaves

2.5 cm (1 in) fresh root ginger, cut into juliennes

200 g (7 oz) onions, sliced

2 green chillies, slit lengthways

2 potatoes, peeled and cut into 1 cm (1/2 in) dice

2 carrots, peeled and cut into 1 cm (1/2 in) dice

150 g (5 oz) cauliflower, cut into small florets

500 ml (18 fl oz) coconut milk

150 g (5 oz) peas, thawed if frozen

1 teaspoon sugar

salt, to taste

20 g (3/4 oz) rice flour

fried curry leaves, to garnish

Heat the oil in a large pan and when hot, add the mustard seeds. When they begin to crackle, add the curry leaves, ginger juliennes and sliced onions. Cook, stirring, for 5 minutes and then add the green chillies. Add the potatoes, carrots and cauliflower and stir together.

Pour the coconut milk into the pan and add the peas. Cook for 10–15 minutes or until the vegetables are tender. Add the sugar and salt.

Mix the rice flour with 100 ml (3 1/2 fl oz) water and use to thicken the sauce. Add a little at a time, stirring all the time until the sauce is the consistency of thin cream. Garnish with fried curry leaves and serve immediately.

Dindigul biryani
Vegetable biryani

This dish is from Dindigul, in southern India. Dindigul prides itself on its very own biryani recipe, which is sold from stalls on the streets.

Serves 4–6

250 g (9 oz) basmati rice
5 tablespoons vegetable oil
3 cloves
3 cardamom pods
125 g (4½ oz) onions, sliced
1 tablespoon garlic pulp
2 teaspoons ginger pulp
¾ teaspoon red chilli powder
2 teaspoons ground coriander
1 teaspoon ground fennel
200 g (7 oz) tomatoes, chopped
75 g (3 oz) carrots, cut into 2.5 cm (1 in) lengths
75 g (3 oz) green beans, cut into 2.5 cm (1 in) lengths
100 g (4 oz) cauliflower florets
100 ml (3½ fl oz) coconut milk
salt, to taste
3 tablespoons chopped fresh coriander
fried curry leaves and plain boiled rice, to garnish

Wash the rice in several changes of water. Leave to soak in a large pan of water.

Heat the oil in a large pan and add the cloves and cardamom pods. After 1 minute add the sliced onions and fry for 10–15 minutes until the onions are soft and change colour.

Stir in the garlic, ginger and the ground spices. Sprinkle with water and cook, stirring, for 5–10 minutes. Add the chopped tomatoes and continue to cook over a moderate heat for 5–8 minutes until the oil begins to separate.

Drain the rice and add to the pan with the carrots, green beans and cauliflower florets. Cook, stirring, for 2 minutes. Add the coconut milk and sufficient water to cover the rice by 1 cm (½ in). Season and stir in the chopped coriander. Cover, reduce the heat and simmer for 15 minutes until the water has been absorbed.

Transfer to a serving dish and garnish with fried curry leaves and a few grains of plain boiled rice.

Ras gobi dhana shaak

Cauliflower with fresh coriander and tomato

This dish comes from Bombay in western India, where I grew up. My grandmother's cook taught me this recipe – it is one of the first things I learnt to cook.

Serves 4

1 tablespoon vegetable oil
1 teaspoon black mustard seeds
3 tomatoes, chopped into large chunks
1 tablespoon ground coriander
1/2 tablespoon ground cumin
1/2 teaspoon ground turmeric
2 tablespoons Coriander, chilli, garlic and ginger paste (see page 20)
900 g (2 lb) cauliflower, cut into florets
3 tablespoons chopped fresh coriander
salt, to taste

Heat the vegetable oil in a large pan, karhai or wok. When the oil just begins to smoke add the mustard seeds. Keep a splatter lid ready so that the seeds do not start jumping out of the pan.

Immediately add the tomatoes, ground coriander, ground cumin and ground turmeric and the Coriander, chilli, garlic and ginger paste. Cover and cook gently for 2 minutes, or until the tomatoes have softened.

Add the cauliflower, chopped coriander and 200 ml (7 fl oz) water. Stir well, cover and cook for 5 minutes. Remove the lid and cook over a medium heat for a further 2 minutes. Season and serve immediately.

◇ **My tip** I always use the stalks of the coriander herb as well as the leaves as it adds a lot of flavour to the dish. I don't like waste!

Left: **Vegetable biryani**

Makai jalfrezi

Babycorn jalfrezi

Babycorn is a relatively new vegetable to India but it is now grown extensively around Calcutta, where this dish comes from. As you travel further north up the river Ganges the flavours change.

Serves 4

400 g (14 oz) babycorn, slit lengthways
300 g (11 oz) tomatoes
2½ tablespoons vegetable oil
¼ teaspoon cumin seeds
250 g (9 oz) onions, finely sliced
½ teaspoon garlic pulp
2.5 cm (1 in) fresh root ginger, chopped
1 green chilli, finely chopped
¾ teaspoon red chilli powder
½ teaspoon ground turmeric
3 tablespoons tomato purée
salt, to taste
1 tablespoon white wine vinegar
200 g (7 oz) green pepper, cut into strips
1 teaspoon East Indian garam masala (see page 23)
3 tablespoons chopped fresh coriander

Cook the babycorn in boiling water for 2 minutes. Do not overcook them as you want them to be crunchy. Place half the tomatoes in a food processor or blender and process until you have a smooth purée. Sieve and set aside. Cut the remaining tomatoes into strips.

Heat 2 tablespoons of the oil in a large pan and add the cumin seeds. When they begin to crackle add the onions and garlic. Add the ginger and green chilli and cook for 3–4 minutes. Stir in the chilli powder, ground turmeric, tomato purée and babycorn and cook for 5–8 minutes. Add the salt and vinegar.

Heat the remainder of the oil in a separate pan. Add the green pepper strips and sliced tomatoes and cook quickly over a high heat for 2–3 minutes, remove from the pan and drain on kitchen paper.

To serve, sprinkle the babycorn jalfrezi with the garam masala and fresh coriander and garnish with the pepper and tomato strips.

Khumbh palak

Spicy stir-fried mushrooms and spinach

This is a Kashmiri dish, which would be served as part of a main meal with rice and stuffed breads. I often serve this with Lamb in a pickled spice sauce (see page 74). They complement each other because one is mild and the other is hot.

Serves 4

3 tablespoons vegetable oil
1 teaspoon cumin seeds
½ teaspoon garlic pulp
2.5 cm (1 in) fresh root ginger, finely chopped
1 small green chilli, finely chopped
100 g (4 oz) onions, chopped
½ teaspoon ground turmeric
250 g (9 oz) button mushrooms, wiped clean
1 kg (2 lb) spinach, washed and shredded
pinch of dried fenugreek leaves
1 tablespoon single cream
½ teaspoon garam masala
salt, to taste

Heat the oil in a karhai, wok or large pan and add the cumin seeds. When they begin to crackle stir in the garlic, chopped ginger and green chilli, onion and turmeric. Add the mushrooms and cook, stirring, for 1 minute. Add the shredded spinach and cook over a high heat for about 2 minutes, or until all the water evaporates.

Add the dried fenugreek leaves, cream and garam masala and season.

Top right: **Spicy stir-fried mushrooms and spinach**
Right: **Babycorn jalfrezi**

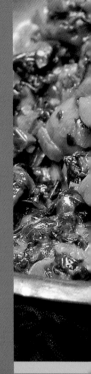

Vattana nu saak

Green peas cooked with spices

This typically Gujarati dish was taught to me by my grandmother's cook.

Serves 4

2 tablespoons ghee or vegetable oil

1 teaspoon cumin seeds

¼ teaspoon white sesame seeds

5 cloves

2 cinnamon sticks

1 teaspoon black peppercorns, crushed

100 g (4 oz) onions, finely chopped

½ teaspoon ground turmeric

300 g (11 oz) peas, thawed if frozen

3 tablespoons chopped fresh coriander

1 tablespoon chopped fresh mint

juice of ½ lemon

1 teaspoon sugar

salt, to taste

25 g (1 oz) fresh coconut, grated

Heat the ghee or oil in a karhai, wok or large frying pan, add the cumin seeds, white sesame seeds, cloves, cinnamon sticks and crushed black pepper and stir-fry for 1 minute.

Add the chopped onions and cook for about 5 minutes until the onions begin to change colour. Add the ground turmeric, peas, half of the chopped coriander, the chopped mint, 250 ml (8 fl oz) water and the lemon juice. Bring to the boil and simmer for about 10 minutes. Add the sugar and salt.

Sprinkle with grated coconut and the remaining chopped coriander before serving.

◇ **My tip** For a slightly thicker sauce, purée about one-quarter of the peas in a food processor or blender and add to the pan with the rest of the peas.

Bhendi aur aloo masala subzi

Okra and potatoes

Okra is immensely popular in Gujarat, where this dish comes from. There are many ways of preparing okra but this is one of my favourites. It is a dry dish, which works well as an accompaniment to a main dish, such as Chicken with fenugreek (see page 58) or with other vegetable dishes in a thali.

Serves 4

900 g (2 lb) small, tender okra

2 tablespoons vegetable oil

1 teaspoon cumin seeds

225 g (8 oz) potatoes, peeled and diced

1/4 teaspoon ground turmeric

2 tablespoons Coriander, chilli, garlic and ginger paste (see page 20)

1 large tomato, chopped

salt, to taste

pinch of sugar

1 tablespoon lemon juice

Wash and wipe each okra with a tea towel (this prevents them going sticky when cooked). Cut the head and nip the end of each okra and then cut into 2.5 cm (1 in) pieces.

Heat the oil in a large pan or wok and when nearly smoking hot, add the cumin seeds. These will start to crackle immediately. Add the potato dice, cover and cook for 3–4 minutes, shaking the pan at regular intervals.

Stir in the ground turmeric and Coriander, chilli, garlic and ginger paste and then the okra. Cover partially and cook over a medium heat for 7–8 minutes. Stir in the chopped tomato and add the salt, sugar and lemon juice. Cover and cook for a further 2 minutes. Serve hot.

◇ **My tip** This recipe can be completely altered by adding 3/4 cup of natural yogurt instead of the tomatoes and some extra salt and sugar. This will give the recipe a thick sauce.

Paneer chaman

Indian cheese in a mint and coriander sauce

All paneer dishes originate in the north of India. This one comes from the eastern state of Bengal. Paneer is quite bland to taste and has a similar texture to tofu, but the beauty of it is that it takes on other flavours well. It is particularly good if browned first, as in this recipe.

Serves 4–6

oil for deep-frying

750 g (1 3/4 lb) paneer, diced

75 g (3 oz) fresh coriander, roughly chopped

1 teaspoon fresh mint, stalks removed

25 g (1 oz) green chillies

300 g (11 oz) natural yogurt

100 g (4 oz) ghee

1 1/2 teaspoons ajowan seeds

250 g (9 oz) onions, chopped

2 teaspoons ginger pulp

2 teaspoons garlic pulp

125 ml (4 fl oz) single cream

1 teaspoon East Indian garam masala (see page 23)

salt, to taste

Heat the oil in a large pan until it reaches a temperature of 190°C (375°F). Deep-fry the paneer until it turns golden brown. Remove from the oil and immerse in a bowl of cold water for 10–15 minutes. Drain and set aside.

Place the fresh coriander, mint and green chillies in a food processor or blender and

Preparing okra

Above: **Indian cheese in a creamy tomato sauce**

Paneer makhni

Indian cheese in a creamy tomato sauce

This is a very typical dish in the Punjab region where paneer is considered a very healthy source of protein. This is a light dish that can be eaten with chapattis or with Lentils with cream and butter (see page 106).

Serves 4–6
500 g (1¼ lb) tomatoes, chopped
100 g (4 oz) unsalted cashew nuts
2 tablespoons vegetable oil
100 ml (3½ fl oz) cream
250 g (9 oz) butter
large pinch of dried fenugreek leaves
½ teaspoon ground white pepper
500 g (1¼ lb) paneer, cut into 1 cm (½ in) cubes
salt, to taste
honey (optional)
single cream, to garnish

Place the tomatoes, cashew nuts and oil in a large pan and bring to the boil. Simmer for 30 minutes then allow to cool. Place the tomato and nut mixture in a food processor or blender and process to a fine purée.

Pass the purée through a sieve and return to the pan. Cook over a medium heat and reduce by one-third or until it becomes thick. Add the cream, butter, dried fenugreek and white pepper and simmer for 10–15 minutes.

Add the paneer to the sauce and add salt. If the sauce is sour add a little honey to sweeten. Garnish with cream and serve hot with a plain paratha (see page 99).

process, adding a little water to make a smooth paste. Whisk the yogurt in a bowl, add the coriander, mint and chilli paste and mix well.

Heat the ghee in a pan, add the ajowan seeds and stir over a medium heat for 10 seconds. Add the onions and cook, stirring, for about 10–15 minutes or until golden brown. Add the ginger and garlic, stir-fry for 1 minute, add the mint and coriander mixture and fry over a medium heat until the fat begins to separate.

Add the fried paneer, stir-fry for 1 minute, then add the cream, garam masala and salt. Increase the heat and allow to bubble for 1 minute and then serve.

◇ **My tip** For a slightly hotter dish, add ½ teaspoon of red chilli powder with the fresh green chillies.

Subzi curry

Mixed vegetable curry

'Subzi' is the generic term for vegetables and is recognised throughout India. I have used carrots, potatoes and beans but in India I would use whatever caught my eye at the market. Karela is a wonderful Indian vegetable that you could use instead of the potatoes (see Preparing karela, below). You need to salt it before using to remove some of the moisture.

Serves 4

3 tablespoons ghee or vegetable oil

150 g (5 oz) carrots, cut into batons

150 g (5 oz) potatoes, peeled and cut into batons

100 g (4 oz) green beans, cut into 2.5 cm (1 in) lengths

4 bay leaves

1 onion, chopped

6 cloves garlic, crushed

2 green chillies, chopped

³/₄ teaspoon red chilli powder

¹/₂ teaspoon ground turmeric

¹/₂ teaspoon ground fennel

³/₄ teaspoon ground cumin

2 teaspoons garam masala

salt, to taste

3 tablespoons chopped fresh coriander

Heat half of the ghee or oil in a frying pan and add the carrots, potatoes and green beans. Stir-fry for about 5 minutes and set aside.

Heat the remaining ghee or oil in a separate pan and add the bay leaves and onion. Cook,

stirring, for 3–5 minutes. Add the garlic and green chillies and cook for a further 3 minutes, stirring constantly.

Stir in the red chilli powder, ground turmeric, ground fennel and cumin and cook for 1 minute. Add the carrots, potatoes and green beans and about 2 cups of water. Stir well and simmer for 5–10 minutes. Add the garam masala and salt and simmer for another 5 minutes until the sauce thickens slightly. Serve hot, sprinkled with the chopped fresh coriander.

Beans poriyal

Green beans with coconut

This dish is from southern India and is very quick to make – it is more of a stir-fry. I use fresh coconut in this recipe but you could easily substitute the same amount of desiccated coconut. It is delicious eaten with a fish curry and plain boiled rice.

Serves 4

3 tablespoons vegetable oil

¹/₂ teaspoon mustard seeds

2 dried red chillies

8–10 curry leaves

75 g (3 oz) onion, diced

1 green chilli, chopped

400 g (14 oz) green beans or mangetout, cut into 2.5 cm (1 in) lengths

salt, to taste

75 g (3 oz) fresh coconut, grated

juice of ¹/₂ lemon

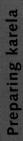

Preparing karela

Left: **Green beans with coconut**

Baingan kalua
Sweet spicy aubergines

Aubergines are one of the most popular vegetables in Indian cooking, and especially in the Punjab, where this dish comes from. You can use the long white aubergines – baby aubergines are also good. This is great as a side dish – perhaps served with an egg curry and a plain paratha or chapatti.

Serves 4
oil for deep-frying
450 g (1 lb) aubergine, cut into 2 cm (³/₄ in) dice
3 tablespoons vegetable oil
¹/₂ teaspoon cumin seeds
¹/₂ teaspoon ground turmeric
¹/₄ teaspoon ground asafoetida
³/₄ teaspoon red chilli powder
2 teaspoons chopped fresh root ginger
100 g (4 oz) chickpea flour
20 g (³/₄ oz) sugar
75 g (3 oz) unsalted cashew nuts
salt, to taste

Deep-fry the aubergine in hot oil for 3–5 minutes until it changes colour and becomes tender. Remove from the oil with a slotted spoon and drain on kitchen paper.

In another pan heat the oil and add the cumin seeds. When they begin to crackle add the turmeric, asafoetida, red chilli powder and chopped ginger. Sprinkle with water and add the chickpea flour and sugar. Cook, stirring, for 3–5 minutes and then add the diced aubergine and cashew nuts. Add salt and sprinkle with more water if required.

Heat the oil in a pan and, when hot, add the mustard seeds, dried red chillies and curry leaves. When the mustard seeds begin to crackle, add the diced onion and green chilli. Increase the heat and stir-fry for 2–3 minutes.

Add the green beans and salt. Cook, covered, over a low heat for 5–10 minutes until the beans are cooked but not overdone. Add the grated coconut and lemon juice, mix well and serve hot.

Thali

The word 'thali' actually refers to the plate that the food is served on, but has now come to mean a multi-dish meal. Originally invented in Gujarat, the thali is one of the most important contributions to Indian cuisine.

Usually made of stainless steel, and sometimes gold and silver, a thali is basically a large round plate with several small bowls, called katoris. In southern India, a thali meal is often served on a large banana leaf. Most Gujaratis are vegetarian so a traditional thali would consist of a number of vegetable dishes, both wet and dry, centred around a small mound of rice. Add some bread, a paneer (Indian cheese) dish, a dal, some yogurt plus, of course, the all-essential pickle or chutney, and you have a complete and balanced meal. The right-hand side of the dish is often reserved for the sweet, which would be served at the same time as all the other dishes. Cutlery is never used – you eat a thali with your fingers.

The thali is a great way to experience Indian food and is served all over India and, increasingly, in Indian restaurants elsewhere. If you like the idea of being able to sample several small dishes, then this is a wonderful way of eating – often the only question you will be asked when ordering a thali in a restaurant is 'vegetarian or non-vegetarian?'. The rest is up to the cook who will prepare for you whatever is fresh and available.

Eating a thali for the first time can be daunting if you are not used to eating without a knife and fork. Indians are very deft with their hands when it comes to scooping up rice and vegetables with their fingers or using strips of bread to mop up the last of their dal. The best way to eat a thali is to get stuck in, eat and enjoy!

Many recipes in this book can be served as part of a thali. Try and balance different ingredients as well as colour and texture. Clockwise, from bottom: Cauliflower with ginger (page 80), Indian cheese in a mint and coriander sauce (page 88), Mixed vegetable curry (page 90), Lentils with cream and butter (page 106), yogurt, Deep-fried puffed bread (page 102), plain boiled rice.

Rice, bread and accompaniments

Rice is the most important staple and has been cultivated in India for over 3000 years. There are numerous varieties – from long-grain white rice to the short red rice, eaten in rural areas in the south. Basmati is probably the most famous variety and I use it in all my cooking – it has an unmistakably sweet aroma and its name means 'queen of fragrance'. Although rice is eaten throughout India, it is more important to the southern diet whereas the north of India relies more heavily on wheat. Bread is served with almost every meal – from the familiar chapatti to the delicious puri, a snack bread that puffs up when deep-fried. Dals, or dishes made from lentils and pulses, are eaten all over India, although the type of pulses used and methods of cooking vary enormously from region to region, so that there are countless variations on the theme. I have included some of my favourite dal recipes here, from Chickpea curry (see page 105) to South Indian lentil curry (see page 106). No Indian meal is complete without relishes and chutneys. Some are exceedingly hot while others, such as raita, are designed to cool down a hot dish.

Above: **Rice growing in the paddy fields of southern India.** *Opposite:* **Local girls working at a pappadum factory in Chennai.**

Tayir sadam

Yogurt with rice

I have had this dish so often but it still remains one of my favourites. My grandmother used to pack me off to school with this in my tiffin and for me it is everything that home cooking should be. It is the one dish I crave when I feel under the weather.

Serves 4

450 g (1 lb) basmati rice, cooked
125 g (4 oz) natural yogurt
salt, to taste
1/2 teaspoon ginger pulp
1/2 teaspoon chopped green chilli
1 tablespoon vegetable oil
1/4 teaspoon mustard seeds
1/4 teaspoon skinned split black
   lentils (urad dal)
6 curry leaves
2 dried red chillies, seeded
1/2 teaspoon ground asafoetida
1 tablespoon chopped fresh
   coriander, to garnish

Place the cooked rice in a large bowl and mash with a masher, adding a little cold water to prevent it sticking.

Add the yogurt and salt and mix well. Stir in the ginger and chopped green chilli.

Heat the oil and when hot, add the mustard seeds, lentils, curry leaves and dried red chillies. When the mustard seeds start to crackle stir in the asafoetida and then pour over the rice and serve, garnished with the chopped fresh coriander.

Jeera pulav

Rice flavoured with cumin seeds

This is a wonderfully simple rice dish that would be eaten every day in most Indian households – it is also very simple to make. I certainly prefer it to plain boiled rice. The cumin seeds complement the fragrant basmati rice perfectly.

Serves 4
250 g (9 oz) basmati rice
1¹/₂ tablespoons vegetable oil
2 cloves
2 cardamom pods
1 bay leaf
1 teaspoon cumin seeds
¹/₂ teaspoon salt

Wash the rice in several changes of water and then leave to soak in a large bowl of cold water.

In a karhai, wok or large pan heat the oil and add the cloves, cardamom pods, bay leaf and cumin seeds. When the cumin seeds begin to crackle drain the rice and add to the pan.

Fry over a gentle heat until the oil coats the rice grains.

Add the salt and pour in 600 ml (1 pint) water, stir lightly to ensure that the rice does not stick to the base of the pan. Bring to the boil and then reduce the heat and simmer, covered, for 10 minutes until the water has been absorbed and the rice is cooked.

If the rice is cooked and the water is not completely absorbed, remove the lid to allow the water to evaporate.

◇ **My tip** To make perfect rice wash 2 cups of basmati rice in several changes of warm water. Set aside for 20 minutes in a colander. Bring the rice and 4 cups of hot water to the boil in a pan. Stir gently. Cover and simmer for 10 minutes until all the water has been absorbed.

Opposite: **Yogurt with rice, South Indian Lentil curry and Black pepper chicken**

Khakhra

Crispy Gujarati bread

Although this is called 'bread', it is actually more like a biscuit that is eaten with tea as a snack. Whenever I go back to India, I almost certainly snack on a few of these!

Makes 8
100 g (4 oz) wholewheat flour, sieved
100 g (4 oz) plain flour, sieved
¹/₂ teaspoon salt
1 teaspoon garam masala
1 tablespoon vegetable oil
100 ml (3¹/₂ fl oz) milk or warm water
50 g (2 oz) ghee

In a bowl mix together the flours, salt and garam masala. Add the oil and rub in. Add the milk or water and knead to make a soft dough. Divide the dough into 8 equal parts and then roll each out into a thin circle.

Heat a griddle pan and cook the bread one at a time, turning once, for a few minutes each side. As you cook each one, brush with a little ghee and pile them up.

Return the pile of breads to the griddle and using a clean folded cloth, press down and continue to cook on the griddle. Turn them over and repeat on the other side. This prevents the breads from puffing up.

◇ **My tip** I find these breads can be kept in airtight containers for up to two weeks.

Chapatti

Indian flat bread

Chapattis are eaten all over India as an accompaniment to most meals – they really are a national bread. The art is in the shaping – a good chapatti should be perfectly round. When I am away from home on my travels the one thing my husband Kirit complains about is that he doesn't get his fresh homemade chapattis.

Makes 10
225 g (8 oz) wholewheat flour, sieved
½ teaspoon salt (optional)
1 tablespoon vegetable oil
melted ghee or butter

Mix the flour, salt and 150 ml (¼ pint) water in a bowl. Add the oil and knead to a soft dough. Leave covered with a wet cloth for 30 minutes.

Knead the dough again for 10 minutes then divide into 10 pieces using a little flour to shape them into round balls. Press out each piece on a floured board using your fingers. Roll out with a rolling pin into thin pancakes about 10–12 cm (4–5 in) in diameter.

Heat a flat frying pan or hot griddle. Cook each chapatti over a medium heat for 30 seconds and when one side dries up and tiny bubbles begin to appear, turn over and cook until brown spots appear on the under surface. Press the sides down gently with a clean tea towel.

Remove from the griddle with a pair of tongs and place directly over the heat/flame until it puffs up. Smear one side with a little ghee or butter and serve immediately.

Paratha
Flaky bread

Parathas originated in the north of India, where wheat is a staple. I love to eat these delicious flaky breads for breakfast.

Makes 6
225 g (8 oz) wholewheat flour, sieved
1/2 teaspoon salt
1 tablespoon vegetable oil
75 g (3 oz) ghee or butter, melted
extra flour for dusting

Put the flour, salt and 150 ml (1/4 pint) water in a bowl and knead to a soft dough. Mix in the oil and set aside, covered, for 30 minutes.

Divide the dough into 6 equal parts and shape into round balls. Flatten and roll out into flat discs about 12 cm (5 in) in diameter.

Smear a little ghee on to the paratha (upper surface only) and fold it over into a semi circle. Smear more ghee over the upper surface and fold it again to form a triangle shape. Place on a floured board and roll into a thin triangle ensuring that the edges are not thick.

Place on a hot griddle. Cook for 1 minute then turn over. When the paratha begins to colour, brush a little ghee on one side. Turn over and cook. Brush a little ghee on this side also.

Cook for a further few seconds until the paratha is golden brown on both sides.

Serve hot.

◇ **My tip** For a quick sweet snack, I like to sprinkle a little brown sugar on top of my chapatti and lightly grill it for a few minutes until the sugar caramelises. You can also add a sliced banana with the sugar and serve with cream.

Roomali roti
Handkerchief-thin bread

Roomali roti is eaten mainly in the north of India. Roomali means 'handkerchief' – the dough is rolled out until it is paper thin and then cooked over an upturned karhai. It is a little fiddly to make but the end result is truly worth it.

Makes 6
175 g (6 oz) plain flour, sieved
50 g (2 oz) wholewheat flour, sieved
1 teaspoon salt
1 teaspoon sugar
2 tablespoons melted ghee or vegetable oil
1 egg
milk or water for kneading

Place the flours, salt and sugar in a bowl. Rub in the ghee or oil. Break in the egg and slowly add the milk or water to form a soft dough. Keep covered for 30 minutes. The dough should be very smooth and elastic. Shape into 6 balls and roll out evenly so they are as thin as tissue paper.

Heat an upturned karhai over a gas flame and cook each roti on the curved base of the pan for 1 minute. Fold like a handkerchief and serve.

◇ **My tip** Making this roti requires a little practice. Start by making a good elastic dough, which can be rolled out very thinly.

Methi thepla

Chickpea flour pancakes with fenugreek

This dish is originally part of a staple diet eaten by Gujarati farmers and taken out into the fields. It is best when accompanied by plain yogurt and sliced onions. I like to reheat any leftover pancakes and eat them with ginger tea. The chillies are optional in this recipe. If you don't want hot pancakes, simply leave them out.

Makes 8

125 g (4¹/₂ oz) chickpea flour, sieved
100 g (4 oz) plain flour, sieved
1 teaspoon ground cumin
¹/₄ teaspoon ground asafoetida
¹/₂ teaspoon ground turmeric
¹/₂ teaspoon salt
1 teaspoon grated fresh root ginger
1 small green chilli, chopped (optional)
1 tablespoon finely chopped fresh coriander
50 g (2 oz) fresh fenugreek, finely chopped
1 tablespoon vegetable oil
ghee or butter, to smear

Place the sieved flours, ground cumin, asafoetida, ground turmeric and salt in a bowl. Add the grated ginger, green chilli, if using, fresh coriander and fenugreek. Add enough water to make a soft dough and then mix in the oil. Set aside for 10 minutes.

Divide the dough into 8 equal portions and roll out into discs about 10 cm (4 in) in diameter.

Pour a little oil or ghee on to a hot griddle. Cook the pancakes for about 1 minute and then turn over and cook the other side until brown specks appear on the surface. Brush with ghee or butter then remove after a few more seconds and serve.

◇ **My tip** I sometimes add ¹/₂ teaspoon sesame seeds to the mixture. As an alternative, you can also use 100 g (4 oz) grated pumpkin or doodhi (see page 108) instead of the fenugreek leaves. Take care to squeeze out any excess moisture before adding it to the flour or the dough will become too wet.

Uttappam

Flat rice bread from Southern India

Although I call this a bread, it is actually more like a thick, round pancake, eaten as a snack. The fresh chillies, tomatoes and coriander add colour and a fresh taste. You can seed the chillies if you want less heat.

Makes 8

225 g (8 oz) basmati rice

100 g (4 oz) white lentils

salt, to taste

1 teaspoon sugar

1/2 teaspoon bicarbonate of soda

100 g (4 oz) onions, chopped

100 g (4 oz) tomatoes, skinned, seeded and diced

1 green chilli, chopped

25 g (1 oz) fresh coriander, chopped

ghee or oil, as desired

Wash the rice and lentils separately in several changes of water. Leave each to soak in a large pan of clean water for a couple of hours.

Drain the rice and place in a food processor or blender and grind to a smooth paste. Add a little water to form a thick batter. Do the same with the lentils.

Add the salt, sugar and bicarbonate of soda to the rice batter and mix well. Stir in the white lentil batter. Mix well and set aside to ferment for at least 12–15 hours.

Place the chopped onion, diced tomatoes, chopped green chilli and chopped coriander in separate bowls.

Heat a griddle or non-stick pan, brush with a little ghee or oil and pour in 2–3 tablespoons of the batter. Spread evenly with the back of a spoon into a thick circle 10 cm (4 in) in diameter.

Garnish the surface with a little of each of the onion, tomato, green chilli and chopped coriander and spread evenly. Sprinkle some oil or ghee over and around the bread. Cook over a low heat until small bubbles appear on the surface, about 5 minutes.

Turn over and cook the other side until crisp and golden. Alternatively, you can finish it off under a hot grill for 1–2 minutes. Serve hot with South Indian lentil curry (see page 106).

Khasta roti

Indian puffed bread

This superb, soft bread is not really an everyday bread – it is something you would make only on special occasions. It is a little time-consuming to make but if you offer this to your guests, they will love it and know that you have gone to a lot of trouble to please them.

Makes 6
225 g (8 oz) wholewheat flour, sieved
1 teaspoon baking powder
1/2 teaspoon salt
100 g (4 oz) ghee, melted
11/2 teaspoons cumin seeds
100 ml (31/2 fl oz) milk
2 eggs, beaten

Mix together the flour, baking powder, salt, ghee and cumin seeds in a bowl. Mix well, rubbing the ghee into the flour. Make into a dough by mixing in the milk and the beaten eggs. Set aside, covered, for 20 minutes.

Divide the dough into 6 equal parts and shape into round balls. Roll out each of the rounds into a flat cake about 12 cm (5 in) in diameter.

Cook over a hot griddle for 1 minute on one side and then turn over. Cook for another minute. Continue cooking on both sides by turning over frequently until cooked, about 5–10 minutes. Serve immediately while still crisp and hot.

Sada puri

Deep-fried puffed bread

Puris are delicious discs of dough that puff up when deep-fried (see below). They are often eaten as snacks or as accompaniments to meat or vegetable dishes. They are also great fun to make and children love seeing the dough circles puff up as they cook.

Makes 20
225 g (8 oz) wholewheat flour, sieved
1 teaspoon salt
50 g (2 oz) semolina
11/2 tablespoons oil or melted ghee
vegetable oil for deep-frying

Place the flour, salt and semolina in a bowl. Warm the oil or ghee and rub into the flour. Adding a little water at a time, knead to make a stiff dough. Cover with a damp cloth and set aside for 30 minutes.

Knead the dough again and divide into 20 equal portions. Shape into balls in the palm of your hand and roll out on a floured surface into circles of 7.5–9 cm (3–31/2 in) in diameter.

Heat the vegetable oil in a large heavy-based pan. When the temperature reaches 190°C (375°F), fry the puris one at a time. Gently push them into the oil with a slotted spoon. When they puff up (almost immediately), turn over and cook on the other side.

Remove from the pan with a slotted spoon and drain on kitchen paper.

Frying Sada puri

Palak puri

Deep-fried spinach bread

This is very similar to Sada puri (see opposite) but has puréed spinach added to the dough, giving it a wonderful greenish colour.

Makes 20

50 g (2 oz) fresh spinach leaves, washed
7 g (¼ oz) fresh root ginger
225 g (8 oz) wholewheat flour, sieved
½ teaspoon salt
½ teaspoon red chilli powder
25 g (1 oz) ghee
1 teaspoon cumin seeds
vegetable oil for deep-frying

Blanch the spinach leaves in boiling water, refresh in cold water and drain again. Place in a food processor or blender with the ginger and grind to a fine paste.

Sift together the flour, salt and chilli powder and then rub in the ghee. Add the spinach and ginger paste and the cumin seeds and mix well. Add enough water and knead well to form a soft dough. Set aside for 15 minutes.

Knead again and divide into 20 equal parts. Shape into round balls and then flatten into round discs 7.5 cm (3 in) in diameter.

Heat the vegetable oil in a large heavy-based pan until the temperature reaches 190°C (375°F). Reduce the heat to very low and fry the puris one at a time ensuring they 'puff up'.

Remove with a slotted spoon and drain on kitchen paper.

Gajjar ki roti
Carrot bread

Carrots are a wonderfully versatile vegetable – they can be made into soups, curries, sweets and a delicious bread, as here. I like to eat this bread with natural yogurt for a snack.

Makes 8

225 g (8 oz) wholewheat flour, plus extra for dusting
½ teaspoon salt
100 g (4 oz) carrots, grated
1 tablespoon vegetable oil
ghee or butter for spreading

Sieve the flour and salt into a large bowl and add the grated carrots. Add 125–150 ml (4–5 fl oz) water and knead to make a soft dough. Add the oil and mix well. Set aside for about 1 hour.

Divide the dough into 8 pieces and shape into balls. Flatten each piece with the palm of your hand and then roll out into a thin pancake approximately 12 cm (5 in) in diameter.

Heat a griddle or flat pan and cook the rotis over a medium heat for 45 seconds. When bubbles appear on the surface, turn over and cook until brown spots appear on the under surface.

Turn over and repeat the process until the rotis are well cooked – about 5 minutes. Remove from the heat and smear both sides with ghee or butter. Serve hot.

Punjabi chole

Chickpea curry

This is a dish in the Punjab. It would be eaten with bread, such as Deep-fried spinach bread (see page 103) or Flaky bread (see page 99), as a simple brunch dish or with a lamb or tandoori chicken dish as part of a main meal.

Serves 4–6

250 g (9 oz) dried chickpeas or 240 g (9 oz) can chickpeas, drained
15 g (1/2 oz) ground coriander
2 teaspoons ground fennel
3/4 teaspoon ground amchoor
7 g (1/4 oz) ground cumin
1/2 teaspoon ground turmeric
1/2 teaspoon chat masala
3/4 teaspoon crushed black peppercorns
150 ml (5 fl oz) melted ghee
15 g (1/2 oz) green chilli juliennes
15 g (1/2 oz) ginger juliennes
3 tablespoons chopped fresh coriander
2 tablespoons chopped fresh mint
salt, to taste

If using dried chickpeas, soak them overnight in water. Place in a large pan of salted water and bring to the boil. Cover and cook until soft, about 30 minutes, and then drain.

Mix together all the ground spices and crushed black peppercorns. Place half the freshly cooked or canned chickpeas in a pan and sprinkle with half the spice mix. Heat the ghee until it is very hot and then pour half the hot ghee over the chickpeas.

Sprinkle with half of the green chilli, ginger, coriander and mint. Add the remaining chickpeas followed by the remainder of the spice mix, chilli, ginger, coriander and mint. Finish with the rest of the hot ghee and mix well. Add salt and serve immediately.

Left: **Chickpea curry and Deep-fried spinach bread served with a fresh tomato and red onion salad.**

Sambhar

South Indian lentil curry

This is a very common staple dish from the south of India, where it would be served with rice. It makes a great accompaniment to a main dish and goes well with Flat rice bread (see page 101).

Serves 4

5 tablespoons vegetable oil
3 dried red chillies
5 teaspoons coriander seeds
1/2 teaspoon fenugreek seeds
50 g (2 oz) grated coconut
150 g (5 oz) yellow lentils (toover dal)
1/2 teaspoon ground turmeric
75 g (3 oz) onions, sliced
1/4 teaspoon ground asafoetida
75 g (3 oz) tomatoes, diced
100 g (4 oz) aubergine, diced
20 g (3/4 oz) tamarind pulp
salt, to taste
1/2 teaspoon sugar
8 curry leaves
1/2 teaspoon mustard seeds

Heat half the oil in a pan and add the red chillies, coriander seeds, fenugreek seeds and grated coconut. Cook, stirring, for 5–10 minutes. Set aside to cool.

Wash the yellow lentils in several changes of water and place in a large pan of water. Bring to the boil, add the ground turmeric and simmer for 15–20 minutes.

Put the coconut, chilli and spice mix in a food processor or blender and process to a fine paste.

When the lentils are soft and mushy add the sliced onions, asafoetida, diced tomatoes, diced aubergine and coconut paste and continue to cook for 5 minutes. Add the tamarind pulp, salt and sugar and simmer for a further 2 minutes.

Heat the remaining oil in a separate pan and add the curry leaves and mustard seeds. When they begin to crackle pour them over the lentils and serve immediately with plain boiled rice.

Dal makhni

Lentils with cream and butter

This is a very typical Punjabi dish containing a lot of cream and butter. Don't let the calories put you off – this wonderfully warming dish is very nutritious and high in protein. If you do want a healthier version use oil instead of butter. I could eat this with just about anything, but it is simply delicious with just rice and parathas.

Serves 4

3 cloves garlic
1 teaspoon green cardamom pods
1 teaspoon cloves
1 cinnamon stick
2 teaspoons cumin seeds
150 g (5 oz) black lentils (urad dal)
50 g (2 oz) red kidney beans
250 ml (8 fl oz) single cream
200 g (7 oz) butter or 3 tablespoons
**   vegetable oil**
1/2 teaspoon red chilli powder
salt, to taste
chopped fresh coriander, to garnish

Using a pestle and mortar, roughly crush together the garlic, cardamom pods, cloves, cinnamon and cumin seeds. Tie up this mixture in a 7.5 cm (3 in) square piece of muslin cloth 'bouquet garni' and place in a large pan with the black lentils and red kidney beans. Add enough water to cover the pulses and bring to the boil. Reduce the heat and simmer gently for about 1 hour, adding more water if necessary.

When the pulses are cooked and the mixture has thickened, remove the 'bouquet garni' and discard. Add the cream, butter or oil, chilli powder and salt. Sprinkle with a little chopped fresh coriander to serve.

Opposite: **Lentils with cream and butter**

Dal triveni
Three-lentil dal

There are three types of lentils in this dish –
toover, channa and masoor – hence its name,
triveni, meaning three. It is a very simple recipe
but is absolutely delicious eaten with pilau rice
and Chickpea flour pancakes with fenugreek
(see page 100). The asafoetida helps to
counteract the sometimes negative side effects
of eating lentils in large quantities!

Serves 4

75 g (3 oz) yellow lentils (toover dal)
75 g (3 oz) split yellow peas (channa dal)
75 g (3 oz) split red lentils (masoor dal)
5 tablespoons vegetable oil
1 teaspoon cumin seeds
1/2 teaspoon mustard seeds
1/4 teaspoon ground asafoetida
1/2 teaspoon ground turmeric
1/2 teaspoon red chilli powder
5 cm (2 in) fresh root ginger, cut into juliennes
1 small green chilli, cut into juliennes
50 g (2 oz) tomatoes, skinned, seeded and diced
2 tablespoons chopped fresh coriander, to garnish

Wash the three different dals together in several
changes of water. Place in a large heavy-based
pan and cover with cold water. Bring to the boil
and simmer for approximately 40 minutes until
they are soft and cooked. Set aside.

Heat the oil in another pan and add the
cumin seeds and mustard seeds. When they

begin to crackle add the asafoetida, turmeric and
red chilli powder. Stir in the ginger, green chilli
and diced tomatoes. Cook for 1 minute.

Add the mixture to the boiling lentils and stir
well. Sprinkle with chopped fresh coriander and
serve.

Doodhi chana dal
Pumpkin and chickpeas

This is a typical dish from Gujarat and is a staple
food for farmers in that region. There are many
types of pumpkin but the ones available in the
Indian grocery stores are called 'lauki' or
'doodhi'. This dish is absolutely delicious
eaten plain with chapattis.

Serves 4

450 g (1 lb) pumpkin
2 tablespoons vegetable oil
1 teaspoon black mustard seeds
pinch of asafoetida
1 teaspoon sugar
1 onion, sliced
500 g (11/4 lb) chickpeas, soaked
3 tablespoons canned chopped tomatoes with juice
2 tablespoons Coriander, chilli, garlic and ginger
  paste (see page 20)
1/4 teaspoon ground turmeric
salt, to taste
chopped fresh coriander, to garnish

Peel the pumpkin and cut into 5 cm (2 in) cubes.
Soak in water (if not using immediately).

Heat the oil in a large heavy-based pan and
add the mustard seeds. When they start to 'pop'
add the asafoetida, sugar and onion and cook
until the onion browns slightly. Add the
chickpeas and tomatoes, cover and cook for
about 10 minutes.

Add the Coriander, chilli, garlic and ginger
paste, ground turmeric, pumpkin and 150 ml
(5 fl oz) water, cover and cook for a further
5–7 minutes.

Serve hot with rice or bread.

Preparing dhoodhi

Begum ka salat

Princess salad

This delightful salad is made in many north Indian households where there is a large Muslim population – the word 'begum' is the Urdu word for 'princess', and is often used to describe the lady of the house. It is great as a side dish but you could also serve it as a starter with bread.

Serves 4

100 g (4 oz) yellow split peas (channa dal)

400 g (14 oz) potatoes, peeled

1 pomegranate (see My tip)

4 tablespoons lemon juice

1 tablespoon chat masala

3 tablespoons vegetable oil

1 tablespoon sugar

pinch of bicarbonate of soda

salt, to taste

100 g (4 oz) red onion, sliced into rings

2 tablespoons chopped fresh mint

Soak the split peas in cold water overnight. Drain and place in a large pan with enough salted water to cover. Bring to the boil and simmer for about 20 minutes until soft but not mushy. In another pan, boil the potatoes until tender, allow to cool and then cut into small dice.

Halve the pomegranate and pick out the seeds with a fork. Rinse the seeds and drain. In a bowl combine the potatoes, split peas, pomegranate seeds, lemon juice, chat masala, vegetable oil, sugar, bicarbonate of soda and salt and set aside for 30 minutes for the flavours to infuse.

Serve garnished with red onion slices and chopped fresh mint.

◇ **My tip** You need only the seeds from the pomegranate for this recipe but keep the juice – it is delicious. Be careful when preparing pomegranate – the juice will stain clothes.

Dhaniya pudhina raita

Coriander and mint raita

This lovely bright green raita is delicious as a dip for pappadums, samosas or pakoras. It is also wonderful with kebabs. In an Indian household it would be made fresh every day but you can store it for up to a week in the refrigerator.

Serves 4
150 g (5 oz) fresh coriander
50 g (2 oz) fresh mint
1 green chilli, chopped
4 cloves garlic, crushed
juice of ½ lime
250 g (9 oz) thick natural yogurt
½ teaspoon sugar
salt, to taste

Place the fresh coriander, fresh mint, green chilli and garlic in a food processor or blender and process to a fine paste. Add the lime juice and a little water if required.

Place the yogurt in a glass bowl and whisk in the green paste. Add the sugar and salt.

You can also make it in advance by freezing the paste before you add the yogurt.

Safarchand chutney

Apple relish

Apples are not a traditionally Indian ingredient but, combined with sugar and aromatic spices, they make a delicious sweet and tangy chutney, perfect as a dip for snacks.

Serves 4
500 g (1¼ lb) cooking apples, peeled, cored and diced
2 cloves
2 cardamom pods
1 bay leaf
300 g (11 oz) sugar
a few saffron strands
salt, to taste
1½ teaspoons ground cumin

Put the apples in a large pan with 200 ml (7 fl oz) water.

Tie the cloves, cardamom pods and bay leaf in a 7.5 cm (3 in) square piece of muslin cloth to form a 'bouquet garni' and add to the pan with the sugar and saffron. Cook over a low heat for about 30 minutes or until the apples become soft and mushy.

Allow to cool, remove the 'bouquet garni' and then pass through a strainer. Add the salt and ground cumin. Store in an airtight container in the refrigerator for up to two weeks.

Preparing coconut

Imli chutney

Tamarind and date chutney

This is a really delicious chutney, which is perfect for serving with hot snacks, such as vegetable samosas.

Serves 4

150 g (5 oz) tamarind pulp
200 g (7 oz) dates
75 g (3 oz) brown sugar
4 teaspoons cumin seeds, roasted and ground
1/2 teaspoon red chilli powder
1/2 teaspoon black salt (optional)
salt, to taste

Place the tamarind pulp, dates, brown sugar and 400 ml (14 fl oz) water in a pan and bring to the boil. Cook for 25–30 minutes, stirring occasionally.

Remove from the heat and allow to cool. Place in a food processor or blender and purée to a smooth consistency, making sure there are no seeds in the tamarind pulp. Pass through a sieve.

Add the roasted cumin and red chilli powder and black salt, if using. Taste and adjust the seasoning. Store in an airtight container in the refrigerator for up to two weeks.

Subzi raita

Mixed vegetable raita

This fresh tasting raita is a classic accompaniment to biryani dishes.

Serves 4

300 g (11 oz) natural yogurt
1 1/2 teaspoons sugar
salt, to taste
1 teaspoon cumin seeds, roasted and ground
75 g (3 oz) onions, chopped
75 g (3 oz) tomatoes, finely diced
75 g (3 oz) cucumber, seeded and chopped
1 tablespoon chopped fresh coriander

Combine the yogurt and sugar together with a whisk. Stir in salt and the ground roasted cumin.

Add the onions, tomatoes and cucumber and serve garnished with chopped coriander.

Thengai pachadi

Coconut and yogurt dip

This refreshing and cooling dip comes from Kerala, where coconuts are used in some form or other in a wide range of dishes.

Serves 4–6

250 g (9 oz) fresh coconut, grated
2 green chillies
20 g (3/4 oz) fresh root ginger, grated
1 tablespoon chopped fresh coriander
500 g (18 oz) natural yogurt
salt, to taste
1 1/2 tablespoons oil
1/2 teaspoon mustard seeds
8–10 curry leaves

Place the coconut, green chillies, ginger and coriander in a food processor or blender and grind to a smooth paste. Add the yogurt, mix well and add the salt.

Heat the oil in a pan and add the mustard seeds. When they start to crackle add the curry leaves and then pour into the coconut mixture. Mix well. Serve chilled as a dip for snacks.

Desserts and drinks

Because of the abundance of delicious fresh fruit grown in India, it is more usual to finish a meal with a piece of fresh mango, banana or melon, depending on the season. However, Indians are famous for having an incredibly sweet tooth and have devised all manner of sweets and desserts, often milk-based, to satisfy their sugar cravings. As well as milk, yogurt features in many Indian desserts, along with nuts, dried fruits, saffron, coconut and, of course, sugar. Indians can be very inventive, and sweet puddings are also made from ingredients such as carrots and peas. Desserts are not really made or served every day but are reserved for special occasions such as religious festivals or weddings. Diwali is just such an occasion and is certainly a time when you would offer sweets, often decorated with edible gold or silver leaf.

Cooling drinks are very popular in India, particularly in the north in the scorching summer months. A yogurt lassi is just the thing to cool you down – yogurt is excellent for reducing body temperature, as well as settling the stomach. Some drinks are welcome drinks, others are best drunk after a meal but all of them are delicious and refreshing – enjoy!

Above and opposite: **Selecting fruit in Kerala. Mangoes, limes, coconuts and bananas are everywhere in abundance.**

Shrikhand

Creamy saffron yogurt

In my grandmother's house in India we would make fresh natural yogurt every day but this recipe works just as well with bought yogurt.

Serves 4–6

1.25 kg (2¹/₂ lb) natural yogurt
5 tablespoons milk
a few saffron strands
100 g (4 oz) sugar
1 teaspoon ground cardamom
7 g (¹/₄ oz) pistachio slivers

MANGOES

Mangoes are probably my favourite fruit and if I'm ever in India during the mango season I go mad for them, eating them at every meal, in milkshakes and ice cream but more often just on their own. There are hundreds of varieties but the king of mangoes is the alphonso, which is grown in Maharashtra, where I grew up. I remember pickling mangoes at my grandmother's house – it was a great excuse for a family get-together and was often the cause for lots of excitement. My grandmother, of course, was the only one who knew the secret spice blend – the rest of us were just helpers following her instructions. After a few days the job would be finished and all the various pickles and chutneys would be stored away in huge earthenware jars to last us the year until the next mango season.

Pour the yogurt on to a clean, very fine muslin cloth, bring together the 4 corners of the cloth, tie a tight knot and hang overnight over a sink, undisturbed, until all the whey has drained out.

Place the milk in a small pan and add the saffron strands. Bring slowly to the boil and then remove from the heat. Set aside so that the milk is infused with the saffron and turns a pale yellow colour.

Empty the contents of the muslin cloth carefully into a bowl and whisk in the sugar until it dissolves. Add the saffron milk and ground cardamom and mix well.

Pour into small serving dishes and serve chilled, garnished with pistachio slivers.

Kesari phirnee

Ground rice pudding with saffron milk

This delicately scented dessert comes from Gujarat. It is traditionally served in earthenware pots (see opposite). The yellow colour comes from the saffron.

Serves 4–6

300 ml (¹/₂ pint) fresh whole milk
50 g (2 oz) sugar
a few saffron strands
50 g (2 oz) rice flour
25 g (1 oz) ground almonds
400 g (14 oz) can condensed milk
1 teaspoon ground cardamom
15 g (¹/₂ oz) pistachio nuts, roughly chopped

Place the whole milk in a heavy-based pan and bring to the boil. Add the sugar and saffron strands and stir well over a low heat.

Sprinkle over the rice flour and ground almonds and whisk vigorously until the mixture begins to thicken. Add the condensed milk and stir well. Cook for a further 2–3 minutes.

Stir in the ground cardamom and serve in small dishes garnished with pistachio nuts.

Opposite: **Ground rice pudding with saffron milk**

Shahi tukra

Fried bread steeped in milk

This dessert is very popular in the north of India and was first introduced in the Royal Kitchens. The saffron and pistachios, both prized ingredients, mean that it is a dessert that is associated with special occasions.

Serves 4
4 slices of white bread
oil for frying
200 ml (7 fl oz) milk
a few saffron strands
200 g (7 oz) sugar
few drops of vanilla essence
20 g (³/₄ oz) pistachio slivers

Remove the crusts from the bread and fry the bread in oil until golden brown. Remove from the pan, drain on kitchen paper and arrange in a shallow serving dish.

Place the milk in a heavy-based pan and add the saffron strands. Bring slowly to the boil. Pour the milk over the bread and allow to soak in.

Place the sugar and vanilla in a separate pan with about 100 ml (3¹/₂ fl oz) water. Bring to the boil, stirring all the time and pour over the bread and milk.

Allow to cool then serve sprinkled with pistachio slivers.

Ghee gol rotli

Sweetened bread and butter

Indians love sweet food and this is a delicious snack as well as a dessert. It does have a high calorie content but when I was a child my grandmother was of the opinion that children needed plenty of sugar to give them energy. This became one of my favourites.

Serves 4
6 tablespoons ghee
4 heaped tablespoons jaggery
pinch of grated nutmeg
¹/₄ teaspoon ground cardamom
8 chapattis (see below)

In a bowl mix the ghee, jaggery, nutmeg and ground cardamom. Warm the chapattis slightly.

Spread a little of the mixture evenly on one side of a chapatti and then roll up into a cylindrical wrap. Repeat with the other chapattis and serve immediately.

◇ **My tip** Ready-made chapattis are available pre-packaged in most supermarkets and Indian grocery stores. However, if you want to make your own, see the recipe on page 98.

Rabadi

Strawberry milk dessert

Rabadi means 'reduced milk' and milk-based desserts and sweets are popular all over India. This is one of my favourites – I do not need an excuse to make this dessert and will often eat it as a snack.

Serves 4

3 litres (5 pints) whole milk
350 g (12 oz) sugar
100 g (4 oz) strawberry purée
150 g (5 oz) strawberries, chopped
strawberry slices, to garnish

Place the milk in a heavy-based pan and slowly bring to the boil. Reduce the heat and cook for about 20 minutes, stirring constantly. Continue to heat the milk, stirring every 5 minutes, until the milk is reduced to 900 ml (1^1/$_2$ pints) and has the consistency of thick cream. This should take about 1^1/$_2$–2 hours.

Remove from the heat, add the sugar and stir until dissolved. Add the strawberry purée and chopped strawberries.

Allow to cool then serve in shallow dishes, garnished with a few strawberry slices.

Matar ki kheer

Cardamom and pea pudding

Peas are not normally associated with desserts but I find that they work really well here. I invented this dish when I once had to prepare a dish for some guests at short notice.

Serves 4

300 g (11 oz) green peas
2 tablespoons ghee
25 g (1 oz) cashew nuts, roughly chopped
25 g (1 oz) raisins
1.5 litres (2¹/₂ pints) milk
175 g (6 oz) sugar
¹/₂ teaspoon ground cardamom or a few drops of
vanilla essence
single cream, to decorate

Place the peas in a pan with water to cover and boil for about 5 minutes. Refresh in cold water and drain again. Place in a food processor or blender and process to a smooth paste.

Heat the ghee in a heavy-based pan, add the cashew nuts and raisins and fry for 1 minute. Add the green pea paste and cook for a few minutes, stirring constantly.

Add the milk and sugar and bring to the boil. Cook over a low heat for 15–20 minutes, or until the milk has reduced by half. Add the ground cardamom or vanilla essence and cook for another 5 minutes. Remove from the heat and allow to cool slightly.

Pour into serving dishes and serve chilled, decorated with a swirl of cream.

Bibinca

Coconut milk layered cake

This dessert is an essential part of the Christmas festivities on the west coast, particularly Goa. The number of layers is important – the more layers, the more effort your host has gone to.

Serves 4

225 g (8 oz) white or brown sugar
5 cardamom pods, crushed
150 g (5 oz) plain flour
5 egg yolks
250 ml (8 fl oz) coconut milk
few drops of vanilla essence
100 g (4 oz) unsalted butter or ghee, melted

Place the sugar in 250 ml (8 fl oz) water in a heavy-based pan and heat gently to dissolve the sugar. Add the cardamom pods and continue to heat for 10 minutes. Strain to remove the cardamom pods and set aside to cool.

Combine the flour, egg yolks, coconut milk and cooled sugar syrup in another bowl. Whisk well to make a smooth flowing batter, ensuring there are no lumps. Add the vanilla essence, mix well and set aside for approximately 45 minutes.

Preheat a grill. Take a 15–20 cm (6–8 in) crêpe pan (preferably non-stick) and set it over a medium heat. When it is hot add about 100–120 ml (3¹/₂–4 fl oz) of the batter to the pan using a ladle and spread it evenly on to the pan by tilting it in all directions.

Cook over a low to moderate heat until the top and bottom are golden brown. Add another 120 ml (4 fl oz) of batter on to the top of the first layer and spread out. Cook under a grill until the second layer is golden brown. Continue until all the batter is used.

Allow to cool before turning out of the pan. Cut into tiny wedges and serve.

Lassi

Chilled yogurt drink

Drinking lassi is a great way to beat the heat of the scorching sun in summer. Yogurt has many health-giving properties and this drink is perfect for settling the stomach – particularly after a very spicy Indian meal. It can be served sweet or salted.

Serves 4

400 g (14 oz) natural yogurt
75 g (3 oz) sugar or 1¹/₂ teaspoons salt
1 teaspoon roasted coriander seeds, crushed
pistachio slivers, to garnish

Pour the yogurt into a bowl, add the sugar or salt and 200 ml (7 fl oz) chilled water. Whisk well until all the sugar or salt has dissolved and all the lumps of yogurt are broken down, leaving a smooth flowing liquid. Stir in the coriander seeds and serve chilled, garnished with pistachio slivers.

Panna

Summer mango drink

This drink is popular all over Gujarat and Rajasthan. Green mangoes are quite sour, which is why you add sugar and cardamom. This sweet-and-sour effect is great for boosting energy.

Serves 4

4 green mangoes
100 g (3¹/₂ oz) brown sugar, or to taste
¹/₂ teaspoon salt
1 teaspoon ground cardamom

Place the mangoes in a pan with some water and bring to the boil. Simmer for about 30 minutes. Allow to cool then remove from the pan. Peel, seed and put the pulp into a bowl.

In a separate pan bring the sugar and 250 ml (8 fl oz) water to the boil. When the sugar has dissolved, add the mango pulp and continue to cook for about 10 minutes. When it starts to thicken, remove from the heat and add the salt and cardamom. Dilute with chilled water and serve over ice.

Badaami karboocha

Almond and melon milk

This wonderful drink is invigorating as well as delicious. Sunflower seeds are an excellent pick-me-up and this drink will give you energy.

Serves 4

75 g (3 oz) melon seeds or sunflower seeds
1 tablespoon white poppy seeds
1.2 litres (2 pints) milk
10 saffron strands
2 tablespoons jaggery or honey
1 tablespoon cashew nuts, chopped
1 tablespoon almonds, chopped
3 green cardamom pods, ground (with husks)
pinch of black pepper

Soak the melon or sunflower seeds in water for 30 minutes. Drain and place in a blender with the poppy seeds and 1 tablespoon of milk.

Soak the saffron strands in about 1 tablespoon of hot water for 5 minutes. Heat the milk then add the remaining ingredients to the pan. Stir in the sunflower seed mixture together with the saffron-infused water. Serve chilled.

Nimbu paani

Sweet lime water

This refreshing drink is served all over India during the summer. It is often served as a welcome drink.

Serves 4

75 g (3 oz) sugar
juice of 1 lime
¹/₂ teaspoon salt
fresh mint and lemon slices, to garnish

Mix 750 ml (1¹/₂ pints) water and the sugar together in a bowl until the sugar has dissolved. Add the lime juice and salt and stir well. Serve with ice and fresh mint leaves and lemon slices.

◇ **My tip** Squeezing fresh limes can be hard work. I put mine in the microwave for 10 seconds before squeezing them – it makes it much easier.

Indian cooking for family and friends

quick fixes

There are times when putting together a full Indian meal simply isn't possible and there are plenty of days when all I want is a fast bite to eat. This chapter is all about fast and delicious ways to eat when time is short – perhaps when a friend has dropped by for lunch or when you just fancy a tasty snack to keep you going. The spicy French toast is a great breakfast or brunch dish and takes just minutes to prepare, while my Bombay mixed vegetable sandwich is an interesting take on a classic snack.

AUBERGINE DIP

serves four

675 g (1½ lb) aubergines

2 cloves garlic, finely chopped

1 tablespoon finely chopped fresh
   coriander

1–2 finely chopped chillies

1 tomato, finely chopped

¾ teaspoon salt

1 small onion, finely chopped

1 tablespoon finely chopped chives

1 teaspoon ground cumin

2 teaspoons lemon juice or natural yogurt

1 tablespoon vegetable oil

1 teaspoon garam masala

½ teaspoon sugar

hot naan bread, toast, poppadums or
   crackers, to serve

Aubergines are a wonderfully versatile vegetable – this dip is a particular favourite with my family and friends. It is great with poppadums but any kind of crispy snack will do.

Place the whole aubergines under a preheated grill and cook for 15–20 minutes until the skin is blackened and burnt on all sides and the flesh is soft and 'pulpy'. Remove from the grill and leave to cool to room temperature, before peeling off all the skin and removing the stalks. Place the aubergine flesh in a bowl and mash further using a potato masher or a wooden spoon.

Add all the remaining ingredients to the aubergine purée and stir well. Serve cold with hot naan bread, toast, poppadums or crackers.

Tip To cook the aubergines without having to watch them, wrap them in foil, put them on a baking tray and bake in a preheated oven, 180°C (350°F), Gas 4, for 20–25 minutes.

SPICY FRENCH TOAST

serves four

3 eggs

1 tablespoon milk

pinch of salt

½ teaspoon ground turmeric

½ teaspoon ground cumin

1 green chilli, finely chopped

1 teaspoon chopped fresh coriander

1 tablespoon melted butter

1 onion, finely diced

1 tablespoon oil

4 slices of bread, crusts removed

This recipe originally started off as a spicy omelette until I decided to dip bread in the mixture.

Break the eggs into a bowl and add the milk, salt, ground turmeric, ground cumin, chilli, fresh coriander, melted butter and onion. Whisk well.

Heat the oil in a pan. Dip each slice of bread, one at a time, into the egg mixture, ensuring that the egg coats the bread evenly. Transfer the bread slices to the pan and cook for about 3 minutes over a medium heat until light brown in colour. Turn the bread over and cook the other side for the same length of time. Serve hot.

Opposite: **Spicy French toast**

SPICED MINCED LAMB BALLS

serves four

500 g (1¼ lb) minced lamb or beef

1 egg

2 onions, finely chopped

1 tablespoon finely chopped fresh
   coriander, plus extra to garnish

½ teaspoon ground turmeric

1 teaspoon chilli powder

1 teaspoon garam masala

½ teaspoon garlic pulp

1 teaspoon ginger pulp

pinch of ground nutmeg (optional)

½ teaspoon salt

vegetable oil, for shallow frying

Coriander and Mint Raita, to serve

These are usually served as a snack with Coriander and Mint Raita (see page 110), however I always make double the quantity and freeze half so that I can enjoy them another time.

Combine all the ingredients except the oil in a bowl, mixing well, to make a fairly sticky mixture. Divide into 20–25 balls.

Heat the vegetable oil in a shallow frying pan. Cook 6 meatballs at a time, immersing them in the oil and gently swirling the oil around, to brown them on all sides, for 3–4 minutes. Drain on absorbent kitchen paper.

Sprinkle with coriander and serve hot or cold with Coriander and Mint Raita.

PASTA WITH CURRY SAUCE

serves four

15 g (½ oz) butter

½ teaspoon cumin seeds

1 large onion, sliced

1 teaspoon garlic pulp

½ teaspoon ground turmeric

1 teaspoon garam masala

1 green pepper, seeded and sliced

1 red pepper, seeded and sliced

3 tablespoons single cream

salt

300 g (11 oz) cooked pasta

100 g (4 oz) grated cheese, to serve

My children love this recipe. They used to eat only plain pasta until they saw me changing the flavour of leftover pasta and now they will not have it any other way! Grated mature Cheddar tastes better than Parmesan cheese as a topping.

Heat the butter in a pan and add the cumin seeds. When they begin to crackle, add the sliced onions and fry for 5–8 minutes. Add the garlic pulp, ground turmeric and garam masala and continue to fry over a low heat.

Add the green and red peppers and cook for another 3–5 minutes. Add the single cream and salt to taste.

Add the cooked pasta to the sauce, sprinkle with grated cheese and serve hot.

SPICED BEANS
ON NAAN BREAD

serves two

1 teaspoon vegetable oil

1 teaspoon cumin seeds

1 green chilli, seeded and chopped

pinch of asafoetida

400 g (14 oz) can baked beans

2 mini naan breads

1 tablespoon Cheddar cheese, grated

1 teaspoon chopped fresh coriander

1 tablespoon chopped onions

This very simple dish is quick to make and is an all-time favourite with my husband.

Heat the oil, then add the cumin seeds. When they begin to crackle, add the green chilli and asafoetida. After 30 seconds add the baked beans. Give the mixture a good stir, then reduce the heat.

Place the naan breads on a baking tray. When the beans are heated through tip them on to each naan bread. Sprinkle the grated cheese, coriander and onions over the beans.

Place under a preheated grill and cook briefly until the cheese starts to melt and brown. Serve at once and eat hot.

MASALA POPPADUMS

serves two

1 onion, chopped

2 potatoes, peeled, boiled and chopped

1 large tomato, chopped

2 tablespoons chopped fresh coriander

1–2 green chillies, chopped and seeded or
   ½ teaspoon chilli powder

¼ teaspoon salt

1 teaspoon cracked black pepper

1 teaspoon roasted cumin seeds, crushed
   (see Tip)

1 tablespoon lemon juice

4 ready-cooked poppadums

Poppadums are an extremely popular snack throughout India as well as in the many Indian restaurants outside India. My family loves this fun way of eating them, which they like to call 'Go Crackers'!

Mix all the ingredients except the poppadums together in a bowl and divide into 4 portions. Sprinkle each portion over each poppadum and serve immediately so they don't go soggy.

Tip To roast cumin seeds, place them in a glass bowl or on a plate and cook in the microwave on high for 30–40 seconds. Crush coarsely using a pestle and mortar. Roasted cumin can be stored in an airtight container at room temperature for about 2–3 months.

CHEESE-STUFFED PEPPERS

serves two to four

150 g (5 oz) Cheddar cheese, grated

1 onion, diced

1 tomato, chopped

1 green or red chilli, chopped

½ teaspoon ground black pepper

1 tablespoon chopped fresh coriander or
   fresh basil

½ teaspoon dried mixed herbs

1 teaspoon vegetable or olive oil

2 large red or green peppers, halved
   lengthways and seeded

Serve these peppers as an accompaniment to vegetarian or non-vegetarian main dishes, or as a snack with a green salad. An alternative, equally good version of the recipe below is to use 250 g (9 oz) of leftover mashed potato instead of cheese to fill the peppers, finishing off with a topping of grated cheese.

Preheat the oven to 180°C (350°F), Gas 4.
   Place all the ingredients except the oil and the peppers in a bowl and mix well.
   Rub the oil over the skin of the pepper halves and stuff them equally with the cheese mixture. Arrange on a baking tray, place in the preheated oven and cook for 20 minutes. Serve at once.

Opposite: **Masala poppadums**

BOMBAY MIXED VEGETABLE SANDWICH

serves two

FOR THE SANDWICH

4 slices of good white bread

15 g (½ oz) butter

1 potato, boiled, peeled and sliced into rounds

2 tomatoes, sliced

1 small onion, sliced into rings

10 slices of cucumber

salt and pepper, to taste

FOR THE CORIANDER CHUTNEY

150 g (5 oz) chopped fresh coriander

2 tablespoons mint leaves, chopped

3 cloves garlic, peeled

2.5 cm (1 in) piece of fresh root ginger, unpeeled and washed

¼ teaspoon salt

1 teaspoon sugar

2 green chillies

2 tablespoons lemon juice

This recipe brings back fond memories of my school days in Mumbai. I could never wait for the 11 o'clock break when we used to buy these sandwiches from the hawker stall outside the school gates! It is a great snack to take on picnics and is ideal served with hot soup. Once made, the coriander chutney can be kept in the fridge for up to 10 days.

To make the coriander chutney, place all the ingredients in a blender. Blend to a smooth paste, adding a little water if necessary to ease the blending. The resulting chutney will be fairly thick.

Spread the 4 slices of bread with the butter, then spread each slice with 1 tablespoon coriander chutney. Lay 2 slices of the bread, chutney side up, on a work surface. Top with sliced potato, tomatoes, onion and cucumber, sprinkling salt and pepper between each layer. Top with the remaining slices of bread. Cut diagonally and serve.

SPICED FRIED FISH

serves two

½ teaspoon ginger pulp

½ teaspoon garlic pulp

¼ teaspoon chilli powder

¼ teaspoon salt

½ teaspoon ground turmeric

1 tablespoon lemon juice

2 x 175 g (6 oz) plaice fillets

vegetable oil, for shallow frying

1 tablespoon rice flour

1 tablespoon semolina

I first had this dish, kurmuri tali macchi, at my aunt's weekend resort in Goa and have never forgotten it. It makes a great snack or starter served with some fresh raita (see page 110).

Mix the ginger, garlic, chilli powder, salt and ground turmeric with the lemon juice. Rub the mixture all over the fish fillets and leave for 5 minutes.

Heat the oil in a frying pan. Mix together the rice flour and semolina then dust or pat the fish with this mixture, pressing it on to the fish so that it sticks well. Shallow fry the plaice for 2–3 minutes, then serve.

CHICKEN
WITH GREEN PEPPERS

serves four

3 teaspoons garlic pulp

2 teaspoons garam masala

3 tablespoons vegetable oil

salt

4 skinless chicken breast fillets, each cut
   into 3 strips

2 cloves

2 green cardamom pods

2 bay leaves

1 teaspoon cumin seeds

2 small onions, sliced

1 teaspoon ginger pulp

1 teaspoon ground turmeric

1 teaspoon chilli powder

3 teaspoons ground coriander

200 g (7 oz) tomatoes, chopped

100 g (4 oz) green pepper strips

100 ml (3½ fl oz) single cream, plus extra
   to garnish

1 teaspoon sugar

1 tablespoon chopped fresh coriander, plus
   extra to garnish

When I was growing up in India, green peppers were available only during the months of November, December and January. During that time we certainly had our fill of this dish, known as murgh simla mirch – now I can prepare it all year round.

Place the garlic pulp, half of the garam masala, 1 tablespoon of the oil and 1 teaspoon of salt in a bowl and mix well. Add the chicken pieces and leave to marinate for about 2 hours.

Heat the remaining oil in a pan and add the cloves, cardamom pods, bay leaves and cumin seeds. When they begin to crackle add the sliced onions and fry for 10–15 minutes.

Add the ginger pulp and the ground spices (except the remaining garam masala). Fry over a medium heat for 1 minute. Add the chopped tomatoes and continue to cook over a medium heat for 10 minutes. Add the green peppers and the cream. Add salt to taste then add the sugar and remaining garam masala. Cook for 2–3 minutes then add the chopped coriander.

Cook the marinated chicken in a hot frying pan or under a preheated grill for about 5–8 minutes each side. Arrange in a serving dish and pour the tomato and green pepper sauce over the top. Serve garnished with cream and plenty of chopped fresh coriander.

OKRA WITH ONIONS

serves four

2 tablespoons vegetable oil, plus extra for
   deep-frying

350 g (12 oz) okra, diced

1 teaspoon cumin seeds

2.5 cm (1 in) piece of fresh root ginger,
   chopped

4 cloves garlic, chopped

1 green chilli, chopped

½ teaspoon ground turmeric

2 medium onions, sliced

1 tomato, diced

1 teaspoon ground cumin

juice of ½ lemon

salt

1 tablespoon chopped fresh coriander

This very simple dish, known in India as bhendi do pyaaza, has become an all-time favourite in Indian restaurants.

Heat the oil for deep-frying in a large heavy-based pan to 190°C (350°F). Add the diced okra and deep-fry for 5–8 minutes until it goes limp. Drain and set aside.

Heat the 2 tablespoons oil in another pan and add the cumin seeds. When they begin to crackle add the chopped ginger, chopped garlic, green chilli and ground turmeric. After 1 minute add the sliced onions. Fry over a medium heat, stirring constantly, adding a little water to prevent sticking. Add the diced tomato.

When the onions have become soft but not coloured, add the deep-fried okra and stir well. Sprinkle with ground cumin, add the lemon juice and season with salt to taste. Finally, add the chopped coriander and serve hot.

GINGERY TURNIPS

serves four

1 tablespoon vegetable oil

1 teaspoon cumin seeds

pinch of asafoetida (optional)

1 teaspoon sesame seeds

2 green chillies, seeded and sliced

5 cm (2 in) piece of fresh root ginger,
   peeled and cut into juliennes

450 g (1 lb) turnips, peeled and cut into
   wedges

1 teaspoon salt

½ teaspoon sugar

1 tablespoon lemon juice

pinch of ground nutmeg

Eaten very often in the northern state of Kashmir, this recipe can also be made with Savoy cabbage, raw beetroot, radish or courgettes instead of turnips. It can be eaten on its own, hot or cold, but it also works well as an accompaniment. It goes well with Smoked Lamb with Saffron (see page 210).

Heat the oil in a wok, karhai or large pan, then add the cumin seeds and asafoetida, if using. When the cumin seeds start to crackle, add the sesame seeds. When they begin to brown add the green chillies, ginger and turnips. Cover and cook over a low heat for 15 minutes, stirring occasionally.

Add the salt, sugar and lemon juice. Cook for a further 2–3 minutes. Turn off the heat and sprinkle with nutmeg. Serve the turnips hot or cold.

Opposite: **Okra with onions**

SPICY SPINACH WITH EGGS

serves four

2 tablespoons vegetable oil

1 teaspoon black mustard seeds

1 onion, diced

2 cloves garlic, crushed

600 g (1 lb 5 oz) baby leaf spinach

1 tomato, diced

¾ teaspoon salt

¼ teaspoon chilli powder

4 eggs

1 teaspoon black peppercorns, coarsely
  crushed

1 tablespoon chopped fresh coriander

buttered bread or hot naan bread, to serve

This east Indian recipe is traditionally eaten for breakfast, brunch or lunch with naan bread or 'pao', a type of soft bread roll.

Heat the oil in a shallow frying pan and fry the mustard seeds until they begin to crackle. Add the onion and garlic and sauté until the onion is translucent. Add the spinach, tomato, salt and chilli powder. Cook, covered, over a medium heat for 10 minutes or until the spinach has wilted. Stir well and make four hollows in the spinach. Break an egg into each hollow. Cover and cook for another 10 minutes or until the eggs are set.

Sprinkle with black pepper and fresh coriander. Lift the eggs and spinach out of the pan with a flat wooden spoon and slide on to a plate. Serve with buttered bread or hot naan bread.

TANGY FRUIT SALAD

serves two

1 tablespoon sherry

50 ml (2 fl oz) orange juice

1 teaspoon vegetable oil

½ teaspoon cumin seeds

1 cm (½ in) piece of cinnamon stick

4 cloves

4 green cardamom pods

½ pineapple, diced

1 red or green apple, chopped

handful red or green grapes, halved and
   seeded

1 tangerine or orange, segmented

1 green chilli, seeded and chopped
   (optional)

pinch of ground nutmeg

This is a good snack if you are bored of eating just plain fruit and is a good example of how I like to add spice to just about everything! Surprisingly, a seeded green chilli mixed in with the fruit gives this salad a pleasant 'kick'.

Mix the sherry and orange juice together in a large bowl.

Heat the oil in a small frying pan and then add the cumin seeds. When they begin to crackle add the cinnamon stick, cloves and cardamom pods. Turn off the heat and add this mixture to the sherry and orange juice. Toss in the fruit and the chilli, if using, and sprinkle with nutmeg.

Dinner with the family at the end of the day is a key time for all of us to catch up on everyone's news. Although I am a busy working wife and mother, I strongly believe in the importance of cooking and eating a proper meal with my family. Many people still believe Indian food is time-consuming to prepare as well as being high in fat but this chapter is full of everyday dishes that are not only quick to prepare, but will provide a balanced diet. Choose from simple fish curries and meat dishes to crunchy vegetables and fresh salads.

everyday
family
meals

FLAKY FLAT BREAD
WITH A SPICED EGG COATING

serves four

200 g (7 oz) plain flour

200 g (7 oz) wholewheat flour

1 teaspoon ajowan or cumin seeds

1 tablespoon vegetable oil

150 ml (¼ pint) warm water

4 eggs, beaten

1 onion, finely chopped

1 tomato, finely chopped

1–2 green chillies, finely chopped

1 tablespoon chopped fresh coriander

¾ teaspoon salt

3 tablespoons melted butter

lime pickle or tomato ketchup, to serve

This is commonly eaten by Indians for breakfast. Indian breads are made fresh every day and we were privileged as children to have a cook who spoilt us and served us the bread as it came hot off the griddle.

Combine the flours in a large bowl. Add the ajowan or cumin seeds. Rub the oil into the flour, then gradually add the water to make a pliable dough. Cover the bowl and let the dough rest for 20 minutes.

In a separate bowl, combine the eggs, onion, tomato, chillies, fresh coriander and salt.

Using your hands, shape the rested dough into 8 balls of equal size. Roll out each ball on a floured board into a flat round of 12 cm (5 in) diameter.

Place each paratha on a preheated medium hot griddle or in a large frying pan and cook for 1–2 minutes on one side, spooning over a little melted butter at the edges. Turn over and cook for 1 minute on the other side, again spooning over a little melted butter at the edges. Flip over once again and spoon 2 tablespoons of the egg mixture on top, followed by 1/2 teaspoon of melted butter round the edges. Cook for 1 minute then flip over and again spoon 2 tablespoons of the egg mixture on top, followed by more melted butter round the edges. Cook until the egg is lightly set.

Serve the parathas hot with lime pickle or tomato ketchup.

Tip Shape the dough into 12 rather than 8 balls, if you require smaller parathas. These traditional Indian rolling pins are longer and thinner than western ones, however, a conventional rolling pin will work just as well.

MUSTARD **FISH CURRY**

serves four

4–6 x 150 g (5 oz) monkfish steaks

4 tablespoons French mustard

3 tablespoons desiccated coconut

2 cloves garlic, crushed

1 tablespoon poppy seeds

1 onion, chopped

1 tablespoon vegetable oil

1 teaspoon black mustard seeds

100 ml (3½ fl oz) canned coconut milk

1 tablespoon ground coriander

2 teaspoons ginger pulp

½ teaspoon salt

½ teaspoon sugar

2 tomatoes, diced

coarsely crushed black mustard seeds
   and watercress leaves, to garnish

This curry, known in India as reshmi rai maach, is absolutely heavenly served with steamed basmati rice and poppadums. The mustard seeds and watercress give it a lovely hot, peppery flavour.

Rub the monkfish steaks all over with the French mustard.

Place the desiccated coconut, garlic, poppy seeds and onion in a food processor or blender and work until smooth, adding a little water if necessary to ease the blending.

Heat the oil in a pan. Add the mustard seeds and stir until they 'pop' then add the blended mixture and fry gently for 2–3 minutes. Add the coconut milk, ground coriander, ginger, salt and sugar and cook for a further 10 minutes. Add the fish to the pan and cook for 5–8 minutes. Stir in the tomatoes and turn off the heat.

Sprinkle with coarsely crushed mustard seeds and watercress and serve hot.

FISH IN A **TANGY MINTY** SAUCE

serves four

4 large cod steaks, about 675 g (1½ lb)
    total weight

½ teaspoon garam masala

1 teaspoon salt

500 g (1¼ lb) chopped fresh coriander

8–10 small radishes

2 large cloves garlic

2 green chillies, seeded

1 tomato, chopped

12–14 mint leaves

½ teaspoon ginger pulp

1 tablespoon lemon juice

½ teaspoon sugar

1 tablespoon vegetable oil

This is an exceptional dish which is suitable not only as a quick tasty meal on a weekday but also for entertaining. If you are serving this for a dinner party, you can make the paste for the sauce in advance.

Smear the cod steaks with a mixture of garam masala, salt and fresh coriander. Set aside for 12–15 minutes.

Put the remaining ingredients, except the oil, in a food processor or blender and blend to form a smooth paste.

Heat the oil in a deep frying pan. Cook the fish on each side for 3–4 minutes, then pour the puréed sauce mixture over the top. Cover and cook for 10 minutes over a medium heat. Serve while still hot.

CRISPY **COCONUT PRAWNS**
WITH TANGY MANGO SAUCE

serves four

2 tablespoons cornflour

¾ teaspoon salt

½ teaspoon ground black pepper

750 g (1 lb 11 oz) raw king prawns (thawed
    weight if frozen), peeled and deveined

2 egg whites, lightly beaten

100 g (4 oz) desiccated coconut

vegetable oil, for deep-frying

FOR THE MANGO SAUCE

I ripe mango, peeled and chopped

3 tablespoons mayonnaise

3 tablespoons sweet mango chutney

Opposite: **Fish in a tangy minty sauce**

I am always tempted to make this recipe whenever I see king prawns at my local fishmonger's. It is great as a starter and absolutely delicious as a snack.

Season the cornflour with the salt and pepper. Dust or toss the peeled king prawns in the cornflour. Dip each cornflour-dusted prawn in the egg white and then roll in the desiccated coconut.

Heat the oil for deep-frying in a large heavy-based pan to 190°C (350°F). While the oil is heating combine the ingredients for the mango sauce in a blender and work to a purée. Place in a serving dish.

When the oil is hot deep-fry a few prawns at a time for 2–3 minutes until golden or light brown. Keep warm while you cook the remaining prawns. Serve hot with the mango sauce.

DRY **SPICED** CHICKEN

serves four

2 tablespoons vegetable oil

1 teaspoon cumin seeds

½ teaspoon fennel seeds

1 bay leaf

2 medium onions, sliced

3 teaspoons ground coriander

1 teaspoon chilli powder

1 teaspoon garam masala

1 teaspoon ground turmeric

350 g (12 oz) chicken, cut into 4 cm
(1½ in) pieces

2 green chillies, slit

½ teaspoon black peppercorns, crushed

salt

1 tablespoon chopped fresh coriander,
to garnish

*This is a great chicken dish for picnics as there is no sauce and
therefore no fear of spillages. It has become a family favourite.*

Heat the oil in a pan. Add the cumin seeds, fennel seeds and
bay leaf. When they begin to crackle add the sliced onions and
fry for 10–15 minutes over a low heat.

Add the ground coriander, chilli powder, garam masala and
ground turmeric. Sprinkle with a little water and continue to
fry over a low heat.

Add the diced chicken and green chillies and fry, stirring
continuously. Sprinkle with more water if required. Reduce the
heat and cook, covered, for 10–15 minutes.

Add the crushed black peppercorns and salt to taste. Remove
the lid and reduce any excess moisture by increasing the heat,
stirring all the time. Serve garnished with fresh coriander.

CHICKEN WITH **PEANUTS**

serves four

½ teaspoon whole fenugreek seeds

2 tablespoons vegetable or sunflower oil

900 g (2 lb) chicken thighs or drumsticks, skinned

1 large onion, chopped

1 tablespoon sesame seeds

1 teaspoon freshly cracked black pepper

1 teaspoon ginger pulp

2 large tomatoes, chopped

1 tablespoon ground coriander

½ tablespoon ground cumin

¾ teaspoon ground turmeric

¾ teaspoon chilli powder or paprika

200 g (7 oz) unsalted peanuts, shelled and skinned

1 teaspoon salt

½ teaspoon sugar

2 tablespoons spring onions, chopped, to garnish (optional)

Although the Indian state of Gujarat is primarily vegetarian and has a large non-meat-eating community, there still remain some Muslims who eat meat in certain parts of this state. Groundnuts, or peanuts, grow plentifully and are eaten in a variety of dishes. Groundnut oil was traditionally used in this recipe but I use vegetable or sunflower oil instead.

Soak the fenugreek seeds in warm water for 15 minutes.

Heat the oil in a pan then sear the chicken until browned all over. Remove the chicken and drain on absorbent kitchen paper.

In the same oil, fry the onion and cook until translucent. Add the sesame seeds and cook until brown. Add the cracked black pepper, ginger, tomatoes, ground coriander, ground cumin, ground turmeric, chilli powder and peanuts.

Return the chicken to the pan. Cover and cook for 20 minutes. You may need to add a little water if the chicken begins to stick to the pan.

Stir in the salt, sugar and soaked fenugreek seeds. Serve garnished with chopped spring onions, if liked.

SPICED MINCE WITH SPINACH

serves four

1 teaspoon vegetable oil

2–4 bay leaves

2–3 black cardamom pods, slightly opened

1 onion, sliced

450 g (1 lb) minced lamb or beef

½ teaspoon ground turmeric

1 teaspoon ground coriander

1 teaspoon ginger pulp

1 tomato, chopped

1 teaspoon mint sauce, or 4–5 mint leaves

½ teaspoon ground cardamom

1 teaspoon garam masala

1 teaspoon salt

½ teaspoon sugar

300 g (11 oz) baby leaf spinach

sliced fried onions, to garnish

Traditionally made with minced lamb or mutton, minced beef is now often substituted in this dish. It is commonly eaten throughout northern India. Serve the dish hot with pilau rice or naan bread.

Heat the oil in a pan. Add the bay leaves and black cardamom pods. After 2–3 seconds, add the sliced onion and cook until translucent. Add the mince, reduce the heat and cook for 10 minutes, stirring to brown the meat evenly. Add the ground turmeric, ground coriander, ginger and tomato.

Continue cooking, covered, for another 10 minutes. Add the mint sauce or mint leaves, ground cardamom, garam masala, salt and sugar. Stir well then fold the whole baby spinach leaves into the mince. Cover and cook for a further 3–4 minutes before serving, garnished with sliced fried onions.

GINGERED POTATOES
AND ONIONS

serves four

1 tablespoon vegetable oil

1 teaspoon black mustard seeds

1 teaspoon cumin seeds

450 g (1 lb) potatoes, peeled and diced

1 onion, cut into large dice

½ teaspoon ground turmeric

1 tablespoon ground coriander

1 teaspoon ground cumin

½ teaspoon chilli powder

2.5 cm (1 in) piece of fresh root ginger,
    peeled and cut into juliennes

1½ teaspoons salt

1 teaspoon sugar

1 tablespoon lemon juice

1 tomato, chopped, to garnish

chopped fresh coriander, to garnish

This dish is a favourite throughout India, known as garam pyaz aloo. It is served with hot naan bread or chapattis. The heat levels can be reduced by using less chilli and mustard seeds. Use any leftovers as a sandwich filling the next day – it is wonderful in toasted sandwiches.

Heat the oil in a wok or deep frying pan. Add the mustard seeds and stir until they 'pop', then add the cumin seeds. When they begin to crackle add the diced potatoes, onion and all the ground spices. Cover, reduce the heat and allow to cook for 12–15 minutes. Add a little water if the vegetables start sticking to the pan.

Add the ginger, salt and sugar to the pan. Stir and cook for a further 3–4 minutes. Turn off the heat – the potatoes should be cooked by now. Stir in the lemon juice.

Garnish the dish with chopped tomato and coriander leaves and serve.

DEEP-FRIED SPICED BABY POTATOES

serves four

400 g (14 oz) new potatoes

vegetable oil, for deep-frying

¼ teaspoon chilli powder

1 teaspoon ground roasted cumin seeds
   (see page 14)

juice of ½ lemon

1 tablespoon chopped fresh coriander

½ teaspoon paprika

½ teaspoon sugar

salt and pepper, to taste (optional)

TO SERVE (OPTIONAL)

natural yogurt

Coriander and Mint Raita (see page 110)

I make this when I have leftover cooked new potatoes – it makes a very good starter or accompaniment.

If you are using uncooked potatoes, boil them in their skins until they are cooked. Drain and allow to cool. When cool, hold each potato in your hands and press to flatten slightly.

Heat the oil for deep-frying in a large heavy-based pan to 180°C (350°F). Add the potatoes to the hot oil and deep-fry for 10–15 minutes until golden brown and crisp.

Remove from the oil and drain on absorbent kitchen paper. Place in a bowl, add the remaining ingredients to the potatoes and mix well. Serve hot, drizzled with a little natural yogurt, if liked, and accompanied by Coriander and Mint Raita.

SPICY SCRAMBLED EGGS

serves four

6 large eggs

50 ml (2 fl oz) milk

¼ teaspoon salt

1 tablespoon melted butter

1 tablespoon vegetable oil

1 teaspoon cumin seeds

1 green chilli, diced

1 onion, finely diced

½ teaspoon ginger pulp

¼ teaspoon ground turmeric

1 tomato, diced

2 tablespoons chopped fresh coriander

1 tablespoon grated cheese

This is traditionally eaten for brunch. Originally a Persian dish, it is now served with an Indian 'twist'. The eggs can be served on top of toast or rolled into warm ready-to-eat chapattis, available from supermarkets.

Beat the eggs lightly in a bowl with the milk, salt and melted butter then set aside.

Heat the oil in a wok or deep frying pan. Sizzle the cumin seeds in the oil briefly then add the green chilli, onion, ginger and ground turmeric and sauté lightly. Add the tomato and cook for a further 1–2 minutes. Add the egg mixture and coriander and stir constantly for a few minutes until the eggs are cooked.

Serve the scrambled eggs hot, sprinkled with the grated cheese, on toast or in chapattis.

WHOLE OKRA
STUFFED WITH SPICES

serves four

300 g (11 oz) okra

1 teaspoon lemon juice

2 tablespoons vegetable oil

1 tablespoon chopped fresh coriander, to garnish

FOR THE SPICE FILLING

25 g (1 oz) chickpea flour (besan)

1 teaspoon chilli powder

1½ teaspoons salt

1 teaspoon sugar

1 teaspoon ground turmeric

3 teaspoons ground coriander

2 teaspoons ground cumin

50 g (2 oz) crushed peanuts

½ teaspoon asafoetida

This dish is a speciality from the state of Gujarat on the western coast of India. Stuffing okra sounds fiddly but it is really a very simple recipe – the okra are baked in the oven leaving you time to prepare the rest of your meal.

Preheat the oven to 180°C (350°F), Gas 4.

Clean the okra and make a slit along the length of each.

Mix together in a bowl all the ingredients for the spice filling.

Stuff the slits in the okra with the spice filling, then arrange the stuffed okra on a greased baking tray. Sprinkle the okra with the leftover spices, the lemon juice and the oil and cook in the preheated oven for 20–25 minutes until the okra is cooked.

Serve hot, sprinkled with chopped fresh coriander.

GARLIC-FLAVOURED LENTILS

serves four

200 g (7 oz) yellow lentils

½ teaspoon ground turmeric

salt

juice of ½ lemon

1 tablespoon pure ghee

½ teaspoon cumin seeds

3 cloves garlic, chopped

½ teaspoon crushed black peppercorns

2 tablespoons chopped fresh coriander, to garnish

This dal comes from the Parsi community, based around Mumbai and Gujarat. I often eat it with biryani or on its own as a soup.

Wash the lentils in several changes of water. Boil in enough water to cover with the ground turmeric for about 20–25 minutes until the lentils are soft. Drain and allow to cool.

Place the cooked lentils in a food processor or blender and work to a fine purée. Ensure that the lentils are of pouring consistency, adding a little more water if required. Reheat the lentil purée and add salt to taste and the lemon juice.

In another small pan heat the ghee and add the cumin seeds, garlic and crushed black peppercorns. When they begin to crackle tip the spices over the lentils and mix well.

Serve the lentils garnished with chopped fresh coriander.

SWEETCORN AND CRUNCHY GREEN BEANS

serves four

225 g (8 oz) green beans

1 teaspoon vegetable oil

1 teaspoon cumin seeds

1 green chilli, seeded and chopped

200 g (7 oz) baby corn

½ teaspoon ginger pulp

½ teaspoon salt

2 tablespoons water

2 tablespoons desiccated coconut

½ teaspoon garam masala

1 tablespoon chopped fresh coriander

lemon juice, to serve (optional)

Many people think that Indian vegetable dishes have no texture because of the way that vegetables are cooked in many Indian restaurants outside of India. This dish undoes all those preconceptions!

Blanch the beans in a saucepan of boiling water for 2 minutes then drain. Slit lengthways. Top and tail the beans and cut each bean in half.

Heat the oil in a pan then add the cumin seeds. When they start to crackle, add the green chilli. After 30 seconds add the green beans, sweetcorn, ginger and salt. Sprinkle with water. Reduce the heat, cover and cook for 3–4 minutes.

Uncover and sprinkle with the coconut, garam masala and fresh coriander. Serve hot while the beans are still 'crunchy', sprinkling a little lemon juice on top if liked.

SPINACH WITH CARAMELIZED ONIONS AND SULTANAS

serves four

1 tablespoon vegetable oil

4 cloves

1 teaspoon cumin seeds

¼ teaspoon fenugreek seeds

1 red onion, sliced

¾ teaspoon brown sugar

1 tablespoon sultanas

225 g (8 oz) baby spinach

½ teaspoon garam masala

salt

The first time I had this dish was in Agra, home of the Taj Mahal. Both the recipe and one of the most famous wonders of architecture left a lasting memory. If you wish, you can add a dash of cream before sprinkling with garam masala.

Heat the oil in a pan. Add the cloves and when they begin to swell add the cumin seeds and fenugreek seeds. When they begin to crackle add the sliced onion and brown sugar. Reduce the heat and cook the onion until browned.

Meanwhile, soak the sultanas in hot water for 2 minutes. Drain and add to the caramelized onions. Fold in the baby spinach. Sprinkle with garam masala and season to taste.

STEAMED FENNEL AND GREEN BEAN VERMICELLI

serves four

225 g (8 oz) dried vermicelli, broken into
    5 cm (2 in) lengths

100 g (4 oz) thawed frozen green beans,
    sliced

¾ teaspoon garlic pulp

½ teaspoon ginger pulp

½ teaspoon ground turmeric

3 green cardamom pods, cracked open,
    outer pods retained

2 teaspoons fennel seeds

1 onion, sliced

1 green chilli, chopped

½ teaspoon vegetable oil

¾ teaspoon sugar

1 teaspoon salt

3–4 cloves

2.5 cm (1 in) piece of cinnamon stick

2 bay leaves

250 ml (8 fl oz) water

1 tablespoon chopped fresh coriander

This accompaniment, known as saunf aur sem ki seviyan, is quite an unusual dish, and one that is not normally seen in Indian restaurants outside of India. I first tasted it in Baroda, a city in the state of Gujarat. It is a healthy option for those who are watching their weight.

Combine all the ingredients together in a large bowl and then place in a steaming basket or colander, large enough to fit inside a pressure cooker. Steam for 20–25 minutes. The vermicelli should have absorbed all the water.

Alternatively, put all the ingredients in a large glass bowl, cover and cook in the microwave on high for 15 minutes, or until all the water has been absorbed and the vermicelli is cooked.

Serve while still hot.

SPICY COUSCOUS SALAD

serves four

150 g (5 oz) couscous

10–12 cherry tomatoes, halved

7.5 cm (3 in) piece of cucumber, sliced

1 red onion, sliced

1 green chilli, seeded

¾ teaspoon toasted cumin seeds

1 tablespoon chopped fresh coriander

2 tablespoons lemon juice

½ teaspoon sugar

1 teaspoon salt

½ teaspoon ground black pepper

1 teaspoon olive, vegetable or sesame oil

Couscous has been eaten for several years in India but never in a salad. I experimented with leftover couscous to make this salad and was delighted with the result.

For an alternative version to the one below, drizzle the whole cherry tomatoes and the red onion with the oil and a little salt and roast in a preheated oven, 220°C (450°F), Gas 7, for 8–10 minutes. Add to the couscous along with the juices from the roasting dish and the remaining ingredients.

Cook the couscous according to the packet instructions. Transfer to a large bowl and add all the remaining ingredients. Stir well to combine and serve at room temperature.

SPICED RICE

serves four

250 g (9 oz) basmati rice

3 tablespoons oil

¼ teaspoon cumin seeds

3 cloves

2 bay leaves

3 green cardamom pods

2 onions, sliced

1 tablespoon garlic pulp

½ teaspoon ground turmeric

½ teaspoon chilli powder

3 teaspoons ground coriander

200 g (7 oz) tomatoes, chopped

1½ teaspoons garam masala

2 tablespoons chopped fresh coriander

salt

This spiced fragrant rice is a lunchtime dish but it could also be eaten as an accompaniment. Serve with natural yogurt.

Wash the rice in several changes of water then leave to soak for 10 minutes before draining well.

Heat the oil in a pan and add the cumin seeds, cloves, bay leaves and cardamom pods. When they begin to crackle add the sliced onions and fry over a medium heat for 5 minutes.

Add the garlic pulp and the ground turmeric, chilli powder and ground coriander. Sprinkle with a little water and continue to cook over a low heat, stirring frequently. Add the tomatoes and continue to cook for 4–5 minutes. When the oil separates from the other ingredients, add the drained soaked rice. Add the garam masala and fresh coriander and pour enough hot water into the pan to a level 1 cm (¹/₂ in) above the layer of rice. Add salt to taste and allow to cook over a medium heat.

When the water begins to boil, cover the pan. Reduce the heat and simmer for 10–12 minutes until the rice is cooked.

Opposite: **Spicy couscous salad**

TANGY CIRCLES OF **AUBERGINE**

serves four

2 large purple aubergines, sliced into 1 cm
   (½ in) thick rounds

1 teaspoon salt

1 tablespoon ground coriander

1 tablespoon ground cumin

¼ teaspoon ground turmeric

1 teaspoon garlic pulp

2 tablespoons vegetable oil

1 teaspoon black mustard seeds

TO GARNISH

1 teaspoon roasted coriander seeds,
   ground

2 teaspoons chopped fresh coriander

1 teaspoon lemon juice

As a child khat mith baingan pati was one of my favourite dishes – we used to beg to have this throughout November and December as this was the only time of year that aubergines were available. Now I can cook it any time – I like to serve it with parathas (see page 99) or natural yogurt.

Sprinkle the aubergine slices with the salt and set aside for 10–15 minutes. Gently squeeze each aubergine slice between the palms of your hands to remove all remaining moisture.

Mix together the ground coriander, cumin, ground turmeric and garlic pulp then sprinkle on both sides of the aubergines.

Heat the oil in a wok. Add the mustard seeds and stir until they 'pop' then layer the aubergine in the pan, making sure that each slice is slightly covered with the mustard oil.

Cook for 3–4 minutes on one side then gently turn over with a spatula to cook the other side. Do not cover the pan. Reduce the heat and cook for 5 minutes. Turn off the heat.

Serve, sprinkled with ground roasted coriander, fresh coriander and lemon juice.

BEANSPROUT AND PEANUT SALAD

serves four

1 teaspoon salt

800 g (1 lb 12 oz) beansprouts

100 g (4 oz) shelled peanuts or 200g (7 oz) mangetout or green beans

1 teaspoon tamarind pulp

2 tablespoons hot water

1 teaspoon vegetable oil

2 tablespoons sesame seeds

1 green chilli, seeded and chopped

1 tablespoon pepper, coarsely ground

1 teaspoon ginger pulp

2 tablespoons chopped fresh coriander

salt and pepper, to taste

½ red onion, finely sliced, to garnish

This healthy salad is delicious eaten hot or cold. If you are allergic to nuts or on a diet, you can replace the peanuts with mangetout or whole green beans. Although beansprouts are most often used in Chinese cooking they are also used in northern parts of India.

Bring a large saucepan of salted water to the boil. Add the beansprouts and blanch for 2–3 minutes. Remove from the water using a slotted spoon and place in a large bowl.

Blanch the peanuts or green vegetables in the same water for 5 minutes. Drain then add to the bowl of beansprouts.

Stir the tamarind pulp and 2 tablespoons of hot water together to form a smooth paste. Set aside for 2–3 minutes.

Meanwhile, heat the oil in a pan then add the sesame seeds. When they start to crackle add the green chilli and stir briefly. Add these spices to the beansprouts, then stir in the pepper, ginger, tamarind and fresh coriander. Toss the salad and season to taste. Eat hot or cold, garnished with slices of red onion.

INDIAN **CARROT** PUDDING

serves four

2 tablespoons ghee

6–8 broken unsalted cashew nuts

10–12 raisins

1 kg (2¼ lb) carrots, peeled and grated

1 litre (1¾ pints) milk

75 g (3 oz) sugar

few drops of vanilla essence

pistachio slivers, to decorate

Known as gajjar halwa, this is India's favourite halwa. It can also be made with doodhi, a large Indian courgette.

Heat the ghee in a pan and fry the cashew nuts and raisins over a low to medium heat. When they begin to colour add the grated carrots and sauté for about 5 minutes until the carrots are soft. Add the milk and bring to the boil, stirring well.

When the milk begins to boil, add the sugar. Reduce the heat to a simmer and cook for 15–20 minutes, by which time the milk will have reduced and the carrots turned mushy. Add the vanilla essence, turn off the heat and mix well. Serve either hot or cold, decorated with pistachio slivers.

easy
entertaining

For me sitting down to enjoy some good food in the company of friends is one of life's greatest pleasures. This chapter is about simple entertaining and includes some of my favourite recipes. Some of the ingredients are a little more special while others, such as the spiced puffed bread, look fantastically impressive but these are all delicious recipes which can be prepared with the minimum of fuss.

MONKFISH WITH MUSHROOMS

serves four (as a starter)

1 tablespoon butter

4 cloves garlic, sliced

1 teaspoon ginger pulp

8–10 spring onions, chopped

1 green pepper, seeded and sliced

1 teaspoon chilli powder

1 teaspoon salt

300 g (11 oz) monkfish, cut into 4 cm
  (1½ in) cubes

12 raw king prawns, thawed if frozen,
  peeled and deveined

50 g (2 oz) mushrooms, thickly sliced

2 tablespoons single cream

pinch of sugar

crushed black peppercorns, to garnish

I absolutely adore this starter. Monkfish and mushrooms both have a 'meaty' texture and they complement each other well. Serve with a salad and some warm bread.

Heat the butter in a frying pan. Add the garlic, ginger, spring onions, green pepper, chilli powder and salt. Stir fry for 3–4 minutes then add the monkfish and prawns. Reduce the heat and continue frying for 5–7 minutes.

Add the mushrooms, cream and sugar. Cover the pan and simmer for 3–4 minutes. Sprinkle with crushed black pepper and serve hot.

FISH IN FENNEL AND CREAM

serves four

1½ tablespoons vegetable oil

75 ml (3 fl oz) double cream

¾ teaspoon salt

4 cloves garlic, finely crushed

1 tablespoon finely chopped fresh
  coriander

pinch of ground nutmeg

¼ teaspoon ground turmeric

4 x 150–175 g (5–6 oz) cod steaks

FOR THE PANCH POORAN SPICES

5 dried red chillies

1 teaspoon black mustard seeds

½ teaspoon fenugreek seeds

1½ tablespoons fennel seeds

1½ teaspoons cumin seeds

Panch pooran is a spice blend from Bengal with a powerful aroma. This east Indian delicacy will leave your taste buds tingling. The leftover panch pooran spices can be stored in an airtight container for up to six months. Serve the fish with rice and Mixed Vegetable Raita (see page 111).

Begin by mixing together all the panch pooran spices.

Place 1½ tablespoons of the prepared panch pooran spices in a bowl. Add the vegetable oil, double cream, salt, garlic, fresh coriander, nutmeg and ground turmeric and mix well to form a paste. Rub this paste on both sides of the fish steaks and arrange the fish on a greased baking tray.

Place the fish under a preheated grill and cook on one side for 5 minutes. Turn the fish over using a spatula and cook the other side for 3–4 minutes. Serve at once.

PRAWNS WITH SPINACH

serves four

2 tablespoons vegetable oil

½ teaspoon cumin seeds

2 bay leaves

1 large onion, chopped

1½ teaspoons ginger pulp

4 cloves garlic, chopped

1 teaspoon ground turmeric

2 green chillies, chopped

½ teaspoon chilli powder

2 tomatoes, diced

350 g (12 oz) raw prawns, peeled and
   deveined

150 g (5 oz) spinach, shredded

1½ teaspoons garam masala

2 tablespoons single cream

salt

2 tablespoons chopped fresh coriander

Leafy vegetables, like the spinach in this recipe, are often combined with fish and meat in both the north and south of India. This is a great dish for entertaining – especially if you have guests who don't eat meat.

Heat the oil in a pan, add the cumin seeds and bay leaves. When they begin to crackle, add the chopped onion and fry for 5–8 minutes.

Add the ginger pulp, garlic, ground turmeric and green chillies and continue to fry. Add the chilli powder and diced tomatoes. After 2 minutes add the peeled prawns and cook for 5 minutes.

Add the shredded spinach, cover and allow to steam for 5 minutes to soften the spinach. Stir well. Add the garam masala and single cream and season to taste.

Stir in the chopped fresh coriander and serve.

PRAWNS IN SWEET LIME CURRY WITH MANDARIN ORANGES

serves four

25 g (1 oz) butter

3 tablespoons vegetable oil

1 onion, very finely chopped

3 cloves garlic, chopped

1 teaspoon ginger pulp

1 tablespoon ground coriander

1 teaspoon garam masala

6–8 curry leaves (optional)

2 chillies, finely chopped

1 kg (2¼ lb) large raw king prawns with
   tails on, peeled and deveined

2 tablespoons sweet lime pickle

100 ml (3½ fl oz) dry white wine

300 g (11 oz) can mandarin orange
   segments in juice, drained

salt

roughly chopped dill, to garnish

This is another great dish for a dinner party as the sauce can be made a day ahead. Simply add cooked prawns and heat through.

Heat the butter with the oil in a pan and fry the onion, garlic and ginger for 8–10 minutes until the onion is translucent.

Add the ground coriander, garam masala, curry leaves and green chillies. Continue cooking for 3–5 minutes. Add the prawns and cook, stirring gently, for 5 minutes. Stir in the lime pickle, dry white wine and drained mandarins. Adjust the seasoning to taste and cook for a further 3–5 minutes or until the sauce begins to thicken.

Serve the curry hot on a bed of plain steamed or boiled rice, garnished with dill.

Tip I find that a pinch of salt and sugar highlight the flavour.

BAKED GARLIC AND CHILLI CHEESE OYSTERS

serves four (as a starter)

16 oysters, opened in their half shells

25 g (1 oz) butter

2 spring onions (including green shoots),
   chopped

1 clove garlic, crushed

1 teaspoon very finely chopped fresh
   coriander

2 teaspoons grated mild Cheddar or any
   blue-veined cheese if preferred

1½ teaspoon chilli powder

The Indian name for this dish, samundar ka kamaal, always brings a smile to my face. Samundar means 'sea' and kamaal means 'fascination' or 'wonder'.

Preheat the oven to 150°C (300°F), Gas 2.

Rinse the oysters in cold water and place in a baking dish.

Heat the butter in a pan and add the spring onions, garlic and coriander. Mix well.

Spoon the spring onion mixture over the oysters. Sprinkle with the cheese and chilli powder and bake in the oven for 5–8 minutes or until the cheese starts to melt. Serve hot.

CHICKEN IN A STRONG
GARLIC SAUCE

serves four

3 tablespoons vegetable oil

2 cloves

2 green cardamom pods

2.5 cm (1 in) piece of cinnamon stick

½ teaspoon cumin seeds

1 large onion, sliced

2 teaspoons ginger pulp

3 teaspoons garlic pulp

½ teaspoon ground turmeric

½ teaspoon chilli powder

1½ teaspoons ground coriander

200 g (7 oz) tomatoes, chopped

400 g (14 oz) chicken, cut into 2.5–4 cm
    (1–1½ in) cubes

2 tablespoons single cream

1 teaspoon garam masala

salt

5 cloves garlic, sliced

2 tablespoons chopped fresh coriander, to
    garnish

*This chicken dish is a real must for garlic lovers! Garlic is
believed to have great curative powers, from aiding digestion
to guarding against infectious diseases.*

Heat 2 tablespoons oil in a pan and add the cloves, cardamom
pods, cinnamon and cumin seeds. When they begin to crackle,
add the sliced onions and fry for 5–10 minutes. Add the ginger,
garlic, ground turmeric, chilli powder and ground coriander.
Reduce the heat and fry for 8–10 minutes.

Add the chopped tomatoes and continue to cook over a low
to moderate heat for 10–15 minutes.

Add the diced chicken and continue to cook for 10 minutes.
Sprinkle with a little water if the chicken is sticking to the pan.
Add the single cream and simmer for 5 minutes. Add salt to
taste and sprinkle with garam masala.

In another pan heat the remaining 1 tablespoon oil and fry
the sliced garlic over a moderate heat for 2–3 minutes until it
turns golden brown. Add to the chicken and serve the dish
garnished with fresh coriander.

CHICKEN STUFFED WITH CASHEW NUTS, CHEESE AND PEAS

serves four

100 g (4 oz) cashew nuts, chopped or
  coarsely ground

200 g (7 oz) ricotta cheese

1 teaspoon cumin seeds

1 teaspoon garam masala

1 red onion, finely diced

100 g (4 oz) thawed frozen peas

½ teaspoon cracked black pepper

1 chilli, seeded and finely chopped

½ teaspoon salt

4 skinned chicken breasts

FOR THE SAUCE

2 tablespoons butter

4 cloves

4 bay leaves

2.5 cm (1 in) piece of cinnamon stick

1 onion, chopped

1 teaspoon ginger pulp

1 teaspoon finely chopped garlic

300 g (11 oz) canned chopped tomatoes

½ teaspoon ground turmeric

¼ teaspoon chilli powder (optional)

½ teaspoon salt

1 teaspoon sugar

½ teaspoon garam masala

100 ml (3½ fl oz) single cream

The stuffing for this Indo-Persian dish can be made in advance and stored in the fridge until required.

Mix the cashew nuts, ricotta cheese, cumin seeds, garam masala, red onion, peas, black peppercorns, chilli and salt together in a bowl.

Flatten the chicken breasts using a rolling pin or wooden mallet then spread a quarter of the nut mixture over each breast. Roll up each breast and secure with a toothpick or with meat string tied around each breast.

To make the sauce, heat the butter in a shallow pan. Add the cloves, bay leaves and cinnamon stick. When the cloves begin to 'swell', add the onion, ginger and garlic and sauté for 5–7 minutes. Add the rolled stuffed chicken breasts to the pan and brown on all sides. Add a little water and cover the pan. Reduce the heat and cook for 15 minutes.

Add the tomatoes, ground turmeric, chilli, salt, sugar and garam masala and let the chicken and tomato sauce simmer for 10–12 minutes, or until chicken is completely cooked.

Gently stir in the cream and serve the chicken hot with warm naan bread.

CHICKEN IN
ALMOND SAUCE

serves four

100 g (4 oz) flaked almonds, plus extra to
   garnish

2 tablespoons vegetable oil

1 teaspoon cumin seeds

3 cloves

3 green cardamom pods

1 teaspoon garlic pulp

½ teaspoon ground turmeric

2 bay leaves

1 large onion, chopped

350 g (12 oz) chicken, cut into 2.5–4 cm
   (1–1½ in) cubes

50 ml (2 fl oz) single cream

1 teaspoon ground cardamom

1 teaspoon garam masala

1 teaspoon sugar

salt

1 tablespoon chopped fresh coriander, to
   garnish

This is a great favourite with all my dinner guests, who often request this dish when they are invited round – the fragrant creamy sauce is delicious. Serve with Spiced Kidney Beans with Ginger and Yogurt (see page 172).

Soak the flaked almonds in warm water for a couple of hours. Drain and then process in a food processor or blender to a fine purée. Set aside.

Heat the oil in a pan, add the cumin seeds, cloves, cardamom pods, garlic pulp, ground turmeric and bay leaves. When the spices begin to crackle add the chopped onions and fry for 5–10 minutes.

Add the diced chicken and continue to fry, stirring continuously. Stir in the prepared almond purée. Cook over a low to medium heat for 15–20 minutes.

Stir in the single cream, ground cardamom and garam masala. Add the sugar and salt to taste. Cook for a further 3–5 minutes. Serve at once, garnished with a few almond flakes and chopped fresh coriander.

Tip Why not try this recipe using other nuts? Pistachios, cashew nuts, pinenuts and chestnuts would all work well and give a completely different flavour.

PORK WITH
PICKLING SPICES

serves four

1 tablespoon vegetable oil

**5 cm (2 in) piece fresh root ginger, peeled
and finely sliced**

4 cloves garlic, finely chopped

**450 g (1 lb) pork tenderloin, cut into 2.5 cm
(1 in) strips**

2 tablespoons sweet mango chutney

2 tablespoons hot lime pickle

**2 tablespoons diagonally cut green shoots
of spring onion**

1 teaspoon chopped fresh coriander

*This north Indian recipe lends itself to both special occasions
and everyday cooking. It can be made with either pork or lamb.
If using lamb, get the butcher to cut the meat from the leg into
strips for you. Serve the meat with plain boiled basmati rice
and lentils.*

Heat the oil in a wok and gently fry the ginger and garlic for
1–2 minutes. Add the pork and stir-fry for 8–10 minutes. Add
the mango chutney and hot lime pickle.

Cover the pan, reduce the heat and cook for 5 minutes. Add
a little water if the meat begins to stick. Turn off the heat, stir
in the spring onions and chopped fresh coriander and serve.

LAMBS' LIVER
BAKED WITH **FENNEL**

serves four

2 tablespoons vegetable oil

500 g (1¼ lb) lambs' liver, cut into strips

2 tablespoons fennel seeds

20 g (¾ oz) creamed coconut

50 ml (2 fl oz) water

6 cloves garlic

1 small onion, finely chopped

1 teaspoon ginger pulp

¼ teaspoon ground turmeric

¼ teaspoon black mustard seeds,
    coarsely crushed

¼ teaspoon asafoetida (optional)

¾ teaspoon salt

Liver is not commonly eaten in India but this dish is a delicacy from the 1930s, which I was lucky enough to discover at a friend's house. Serve hot with green beans.

Preheat the oven to 180°C (350°F), Gas 4.

Heat the oil in a shallow frying pan. Sear the liver strips for 5–8 minutes and set aside.

Dry-fry the fennel seeds in a hot frying pan for 2–3 minutes, tossing them continuously. Coarsely crush with a rolling pin.

Combine the creamed coconut with the water and garlic. Boil in a pan for 5 minutes then put the mixture in a blender and work to a purée. Put the seared liver, the crushed fennel seeds, the coconut purée and all the remaining ingredients in an ovenproof dish. Cover with foil and bake in the oven for 25 minutes. Serve while still hot.

SPICED **KIDNEY BEANS**
WITH GINGER AND YOGURT

serves four

1 tablespoon vegetable oil or ghee

2.5 cm (1 in) piece of cinnamon stick

200 g (7 oz) natural yogurt

1 teaspoon ginger pulp

8–10 green cardamom pods, crushed

¼ teaspoon ground turmeric

600 g (1 lb 5 oz) can kidney beans, drained

1½ teaspoons salt

¾ teaspoon chilli powder

1 large tomato, chopped

TO GARNISH

1 tablespoon chopped fresh coriander

1 tablespoon chopped onion

This rustic dish, known as rajma, is popular among all north Indian families, especially the farming community. It is a delicious accompaniment to Chicken in Almond Sauce (see page 168), or serve it simply with plain rice or naan bread and poppadums.

Heat the oil or ghee in a pan. Add the cinnamon stick and stir. After 2–3 seconds add the natural yogurt, ginger, crushed cardamom pods and ground turmeric. Cook over a medium heat, stirring constantly, for 10 minutes.

Add the remaining ingredients and cook for 15 minutes. Garnish with chopped coriander and onion and serve.

LAMB AND POTATO CURRY

serves four

2 tablespoons vegetable oil

2 cloves

2 green cardamom pods

2 teaspoons ground black pepper

2 bay leaves

1 teaspoon cumin seeds

1 large onion, sliced

200 g (7 oz) tomatoes, chopped

1 teaspoon ground turmeric

1 teaspoon chilli powder

1 teaspoon garam masala

3 teaspoons ground coriander

350 g (12 oz) lamb, cut into 4 cm (1½ in) cubes

150 g (5 oz) potato, cut into sticks

50 g (2 oz) natural yogurt

salt

chopped fresh coriander, to garnish

Gosht aloo (lamb with potato) is an authentic recipe that is commonly eaten by non-vegetarian Indians. However, I have adapted it by adding a little yogurt to tone down the heat.

Heat the oil in a pan, add the cloves, cardamom pods, black pepper, bay leaves and cumin seeds. When they begin to crackle add the sliced onions and fry for 10–15 minutes over a medium heat until they turn translucent.

Add the chopped tomatoes, ground turmeric, chilli powder, garam masala and ground coriander and continue to fry for a further 5 minutes.

Stir in the diced lamb, potato sticks and natural yogurt. Add salt to taste and cook, covered, over a low heat for about 20–25 minutes.

Serve hot, garnished with chopped fresh coriander.

AUBERGINES AND POTATOES

serves four

2 tablespoons vegetable oil

½ teaspoon cumin seeds

1 teaspoon ginger pulp

1 green chilli, chopped

4–5 curry leaves

½ teaspoon ground turmeric

½ teaspoon chilli powder

¼ teaspoon asafoetida

400 g (14 oz) tomatoes, chopped

150 g (5 oz) potatoes, diced

150 g (5 oz) aubergine, diced

salt

1 teaspoon sugar

1 tablespoon natural yogurt

chopped fresh coriander, to garnish

I love aubergines and have a whole collection of recipes for this wonderful vegetable.

Heat the oil in a pan and add the cumin seeds. When they begin to crackle add the ginger pulp, green chilli and curry leaves. After 1 minute add the ground turmeric, chilli powder and asafoetida. Reduce the heat and sprinkle with a little water.

After about 2 minutes add the chopped tomatoes and bring to the boil. Add the potatoes and aubergine and cook, covered, at a simmer for 5–10 minutes. Check that the potatoes are cooked. Add salt to taste, stir in the sugar and yogurt.

Serve garnished with chopped fresh coriander.

TAMARIND RICE

serves four

250 g (9 oz) basmati rice

3 tablespoons vegetable oil

2 tablespoons black mustard seeds

8–10 curry leaves

2 whole red chillies

1½ teaspoons asafoetida (optional)

2 tablespoons sesame seeds

1½ teaspoons ginger pulp

½ teaspoon ground turmeric

1 teaspoon salt

750 ml (1¼ pints) water

2 tablespoons tamarind pulp

200 g (7 oz) drained canned chickpeas, coarsely crushed

The combination of rice and tamarind pulp easily gives away that this is a dish from southern India. It is commonly served with fish dishes.

Wash the rice in several changes of water then leave to soak for 10 minutes before draining well.

Heat the oil in a large pan and fry the mustard seeds until they begin to crackle. Add the curry leaves, whole red chillies, asafoetida and sesame seeds. As the sesame seeds begin to brown add the drained soaked rice, ginger and ground turmeric. Add the salt and water and bring to the boil.

Stir the tamarind pulp and crushed chickpeas into the rice mixture. Cover the pan and simmer for 15–20 minutes or until the rice is cooked. Serve at once.

Opposite: **Aubergines and potatoes**

SPICED DEEP-FRIED PURIS

serves four

400 g (14 oz) wholewheat flour
½ teaspoon salt
1 tablespoon vegetable oil
½ teaspoon ground turmeric
1 teaspoon ajowan seeds
½ teaspoon chilli powder
150 ml (¼ pint) warm water
vegetable oil, for deep-frying
mango chutney, to serve

Puris are delicious rounds of dough that puff up when deep-fried. I often eat these as a snack with mango chutney but I also enjoy serving them to guests as they look very impressive.

Combine the flour and salt in a bowl and mix well. Rub the oil into the flour, then stir in the ground turmeric, ajowan seeds and chilli powder. Slowly add the warm water into the spiced flour until it forms a pliable dough. Cover the bowl and set aside for 15–20 minutes.

Divide the rested dough mixture into 16 balls. Roll out each ball on a lightly floured surface into a 10 cm (4 in) round.

Heat the oil for deep-frying in a large heavy-based pan until it is nearly smoking hot – 250°C (470°F). Once hot, reduce the heat to medium, about 180°C (350°F).

Immerse each puri one at a time in the hot oil. Gently push into the oil with a slotted spoon and allow to 'puff up', which happens almost immediately. Turn once and cook the other side for 1–2 seconds. Remove from the pan using the slotted spoon and place on absorbent kitchen paper to drain while you cook the remaining puris.

Eat the puris while still puffed, with sweet mango chutney or any meat or vegetable dish.

SPINACH AND CHICKPEA FLOUR BREAD

serves four

250 g (9 oz) chickpea flour (besan)

50 g (2 oz) plain flour

75 g (3 oz) spinach, shredded

½ teaspoon cumin seeds

1 cm (½ in) piece of fresh root ginger, chopped

1 green chilli, chopped

1 tablespoon chopped fresh coriander

1 teaspoon ground turmeric

pinch of salt

4 tablespoons vegetable oil

This flat spiced bread with bright speckles of green spinach comes from the central states of India. Some people like to eat roti as soon as they are cooked, but I prefer them at room temperature.

Mix the chickpea flour in a bowl with the plain flour and add all the other ingredients except the oil. Add enough water to make a thick dough. Use your hands to work the spinach well into the dough.

Divide the dough into 8 and roll out each piece on a floured board into a flat round of 12–15 cm (5–6 in) diameter.

Heat a pancake pan or griddle. Cook the flat breads one at a time for 2–3 minutes on each side then turn over and cook the other side. Drizzle with oil and continue to cook until the breads are well done, turning the bread over frequently during cooking.

BEETROOT PUDDING

serves four

150 g (5 oz) boiled beetroot, diced

1 litre (1¾ pints) milk

100 g (4 oz) sugar

1 tablespoon rice flour

2 tablespoons ghee

10–12 raisins

10–15 unsalted cashew nuts, roughly
    chopped

few drops of rose essence

rose petals, to decorate

One would probably never imagine combining milk with beetroot, but it makes a vibrant dessert and looks lovely when decorated with rose petals.

Place the boiled beetroot in a food processor. Add a little water and blend to a fine purée.

Pour the milk into a saucepan and bring to the boil. Reduce the heat and simmer for 15–20 minutes. Add the sugar and stir well to dissolve.

Mix the rice flour in a cup with a little water to make a paste. Add this paste to the milk, stirring the mixture continuously as it starts to thicken.

In another pan heat the ghee and add the raisins and cashew nuts. Fry for 1–2 minutes. Add the beetroot purée and cook for 10–12 minutes over a low heat.

Pour the beetroot mixture into the thickened milk and mix well to obtain an even pink colour. Add the rose essence and pour into 4 individual dessert cups.

Serve chilled, decorated with a few rose petals.

COOL MANGO SOUP

makes 1.8 litres (3 pints)

4 large semi-ripe mangoes

1.5 litres (2½ pints) water

8–10 tablespoons brown sugar

1 tablespoon ginger pulp

1 teaspoon ground black pepper

1 teaspoon chat masala (see page 12)

**1 teaspoon coarsely crushed roasted
cumin seeds (see page 14)**

1 teaspoon salt, or to taste

Mangoes are Indians' favourite fruit and we try to make as many recipes with them as possible during the mango season, which in India runs from March until May. They are grown in abundance in Mumbai, where I grew up.

This recipe is a drink or soup, which is mainly prepared in Gujarat households and sipped throughout the sultry heat of the day to keep one cool. Once made, it keeps for up to 4 days in the fridge.

Peel the mangoes and cut them into big chunks. Do not discard the stones.

Boil the mango pieces and stones in the water for 15 minutes, or until the mango turns pulpy. Leave to cool.

Discard the mango stones. Put the mango flesh in a blender and work to a purée. Return to the saucepan and bring back to the boil. Add the remaining ingredients.

The 'soup' is best served cold with ice or at room temperature.

Tip Add a little extra sugar if the raw mangoes are very 'tangy'.

home
comforts

Some days I just want to curl up on the sofa and indulge in some comfort food. For me, this can be anything from a bowl of spicy pumpkin soup to a delicious, warming dal. In this chapter I have included some of my family's favourite dishes, from the spiced cod dish which my daughter loves to fried sweet potatoes with ice cream. Enjoy.

CHICKPEA FLOUR
PANCAKES

serves four

250g (9 oz) chickpea flour (besan)

pinch of salt

½ teaspoon ground turmeric

¼ teaspoon bicarbonate of soda

½ teaspoon ground cumin

1 tablespoon natural yogurt

1 onion, finely chopped

1 green chilli, finely chopped

2 tomatoes, diced

1 tablespoon chopped fresh coriander

4–5 tablespoons vegetable oil

Known as cheela, these thick pancakes are eaten throughout northern and central India, both as a breakfast dish and as a snack with pickles and mango chutney.

Put the flour in a bowl. Add the salt, ground turmeric, bicarbonate of soda, ground cumin, yogurt and enough water to make a slightly thick flowing batter. Stir in the chopped onion, green chilli, tomatoes and coriander.

Heat a non-stick 12 cm (5 in) pancake pan. Pour in a little of the batter, spreading it to cover the base completely and make a thin pancake. Drizzle 1 teaspoon oil over the top.

Reduce the heat and continue to cook the pancake for about 2–3 minutes. Turn the pancake over and cook the other side for 2–3 minutes. Remove from the pan and keep warm while you make another 7 pancakes in the same way. Serve hot.

MEENA PATHAK'S
PUMPKIN SOUP

serves four

1 tablespoon butter

4 spring onions, finely chopped

675 g (1½ lb) pumpkin, peeled and cut
   into 1.5-2 cm (¾ in) cubes

2 carrots, diced

1 teaspoon salt

¾ teaspoon ground black pepper

¼ teaspoon ground green cardamom

¼ teaspoon ground cinnamon

¼ teaspoon ground cloves

pinch of ground nutmeg

300 ml (½ pint) vegetable stock

100 ml (3½ fl oz) milk

50 ml (2 fl oz) single cream

2 tablespoons finely chopped dill leaves,
   to garnish

Often called MKP's pumpkin soup in my family, this came about when I was trying to use up some leftover vegetables in the fridge. It has become the family's favourite soup.

Heat the butter in a large saucepan. Add the spring onions and sauté for 3–4 minutes.

Add the pumpkin, carrots, salt and all the ground spices and stock. Bring to the boil. Cook until the carrots and pumpkin are cooked – about 10–15 minutes.

Allow the mixture to cool slightly before putting it in a blender. Give it a couple of bursts of power, but do not purée it down completely.

Return the mixture to the pan. Add the milk and bring back to the boil. Stir in the cream, adjust the seasoning to taste, and serve hot, garnished with dill leaves.

EASY GRILLED CHICKEN BITES

serves four

1 tablespoon paprika

2 teaspoons garam masala

1½ teaspoons salt

1 teaspoon sugar

1 tablespoon vegetable oil, plus extra for
   drizzling

1 tablespoon garlic pulp

1 tablespoon natural yogurt

250 g (9 oz) skinless chicken breast fillets,
   cut into bite-sized pieces

TO GARNISH

onion, cut into rings

1 tablespoon chopped fresh coriander

few sprigs of mint

This is a classic starter that you would expect to find in a north Indian non-vegetarian household – however I often make these as a snack for my family.

Combine all the ingredients except the chicken together in a bowl and mix well. Add the chicken and mix well, ensuring that the marinade coats all the chicken pieces. Set aside to marinate for a few minutes.

Place the chicken pieces in a grill pan and drizzle with a little oil. Place under a preheated medium grill and cook for 5–8 minutes until golden brown. Turn the pieces over and cook the other side for another 5 minutes.

When cooked, remove and arrange on a plate. Serve with onion rings, chopped coriander and mint sprigs.

DEVILLED PRAWNS

serves four

1 tablespoon vegetable oil

1 onion, finely chopped

2 cloves garlic, finely chopped

¾ teaspoon chilli powder

1 teaspoon paprika

¼ teaspoon ground black pepper

¼ teaspoon ground turmeric

½ teaspoon grated fresh root ginger

1 teaspoon salt

750 g (1 lb 11 oz) peeled raw prawns
   (thawed weight if frozen)

150 ml (¼ pint) water

1 tablespoon tomato ketchup

These delicious spicy prawns are great for cold wintry nights. Serve the prawns hot with naan bread or on crackers with Coriander and Mint Raita (see page 110).

Heat the oil in a wok or heavy-based frying pan. Add the onion and cook until golden brown. Add the garlic, chilli powder, paprika, black pepper, ground turmeric, ginger and salt. Cook, stirring, for 2–3 minutes.

Add the prawns and cook for 5 minutes. Then add the water, cover and bring to the boil. Stir in the tomato ketchup and cook, uncovered, for 2–3 minutes, before serving hot.

TANDOORI
GRILLED VEGETABLES

serves four

1 large green pepper, seeded and sliced

1 large red pepper, seeded and sliced

4 large tomatoes, sliced

1 large onion, sliced

2 courgettes, sliced

10–12 mushrooms

1–2 green chillies, seeded and sliced

½ teaspoon salt

½ teaspoon ground black pepper

2 tablespoons vegetable or olive oil

½ teaspoon ground turmeric

1 teaspoon ground cumin

1 teaspoon ground coriander

10–12 black olives, pitted

10–12 capers

8–10 fresh basil leaves

1–2 teaspoons chopped fresh coriander

FOR THE DRESSING

100 g (4 oz) natural yogurt

2 tablespoons honey

2 tablespoons tomato paste

1 tablespoon vegetable oil

½ teaspoon garlic pulp

½ teaspoon ginger pulp

salt

There are some days when I don't want to eat any meat or fish and it is then that I find this dish satisfying and nutritionally healthy. It is a versatile recipe to which one can add any favourite vegetables or eliminate anything that is not liked. This is my 'personal' version. It makes a good accompaniment to Blackened Spiced Cod (see page 187), or serve it simply with naan bread and poppadums.

Preheat the oven to 180–200°C (350–400°F), Gas 4–6.

Put all the ingredients for the dressing into a blender, add salt to your taste and blend to a smooth paste. Set this aside until the vegetables are ready.

Spread the vegetables evenly on a baking tray. Mix together the salt, pepper, oil, ground turmeric, ground cumin and ground coriander and stir into the vegetables with a wooden spoon. Sprinkle with the olives, capers, basil leaves and fresh coriander.

Cook the vegetables under a preheated grill for 10–12 minutes. Turn off the grill and place the vegetables in the oven for 5–7 minutes.

Serve hot drizzled with the prepared dressing.

BLACKENED SPICED COD

serves four

1 tablespoon fennel seeds

1 teaspoon mustard seeds

1 teaspoon cumin seeds

2.5 cm (1 in) piece of cinnamon stick

1 teaspoon ground turmeric

½ teaspoon ground black pepper

1 teaspoon ginger pulp

1 teaspoon salt

4 x 150–175 g (5–6 oz) thick cod fillets,
  skin on

2 tablespoons vegetable oil

FOR THE SAUCE

1 teaspoon butter

40 ml (1½ fl oz) orange juice

1 tablespoon chopped fresh coriander

1 green chilli, finely chopped (optional)

This dish is a speciality from Mumbai (formerly Bombay), the city where I was born. Cod is my favourite fish for this recipe but you could also use sea bass, haddock or even skate. Serve it hot with a plain green salad or Tandoori Grilled Vegetables (see page 185) and poppadums.

Put the fennel seeds, mustard seeds, cumin seeds and cinnamon in a coffee grinder and blend to a fine powder. Mix the ground turmeric, black pepper, ginger and salt into this mixture.

Dust each fish fillet with this blend of spices. Heat the oil in a non-stick frying pan and sear the fish for 2-3 minutes on each side. Place in a serving dish and set aside.

Make the sauce by heating the butter in a pan with the remaining ingredients. Bring to the boil then pour over the fish and serve while still hot.

INDIAN FRIED FISH

serves four

1 teaspoon ground turmeric

¾ teaspoon chilli powder

2 teaspoons ginger pulp

1 teaspoon lemon juice

1 teaspoon ground coriander

1 teaspoon ground cumin

1 teaspoon salt

½ teaspoon asafoetida (optional)

4 x 150–175 g (5–6 oz) cod or haddock
   fillets

FOR THE COATING

4 tablespoons chickpea flour (besan)

1 tablespoon rice flour

¾ teaspoon salt

½ teaspoon ground turmeric

1 teaspoon garam masala

vegetable oil, for frying

1 egg, beaten

In India something as simple as fried fish can be made exotic, as this recipe demonstrates. Serve it hot with plain rice, Gujarati Dal (see page 197) and lime pickle or have it as a snack that you can eat with your fingers.

Combine the ground turmeric, chilli powder, ginger, lemon juice, ground coriander, ground cumin, salt and asafoetida together in a small bowl.

Dry the fish on absorbent kitchen paper and smear both sides of each piece with the blended spice mixture. Set aside for 15 minutes to enable the flavours to penetrate.

Meanwhile combine all the dry ingredients for the coating, and pour the oil for frying into a shallow frying pan – enough to cover the base of the pan.

Heat the oil. Take each fish fillet, dip it into the beaten egg and then coat with the spiced flour. When the oil is hot shallow fry each piece of fish for 3 minutes on one side. Turn over and fry for another 2 minutes.

Drain on absorbent kitchen paper before serving hot.

SPICED CHICKEN IN A
TOMATO AND MINT SAUCE

serves four

4 skinned chicken breasts

150 g (5 oz) natural yogurt

1 tablespoon ground coriander

1 tablespoon ground cumin

½ teaspoon ground turmeric

½ teaspoon salt

1 teaspoon green chilli, minced

6 tablespoons breadcrumbs

5 tablespoons vegetable oil or butter

FOR THE SAUCE

2 tablespoons vegetable oil

1 onion, finely chopped

3 cloves garlic, finely chopped

400 g (14 oz) canned chopped tomatoes

2 tablespoons finely chopped mint leaves

1 tablespoon garam masala

¾ teaspoon ground turmeric

1 teaspoon chilli powder or dried chilli
  flakes

1 teaspoon sugar

1 teaspoon salt

TO SERVE

Coriander and Mint Raita (see page 110)

naan bread

When my children have friends round I sometimes make this chicken without the sauce and serve it as a spicy chicken burger, with a mango chutney and mayonnaise spread.

Preheat the oven to 180°C (350°F), Gas 4.

Flatten the chicken breasts with a mallet.

Mix together the yogurt, ground coriander, ground cumin, ground turmeric, salt and green chilli. Marinate the chicken breasts in this mixture for 20–25 minutes at room temperature.

Tip the breadcrumbs on to a shallow plate. Lift each chicken breast out of the marinade and gently coat with the breadcrumbs. Heat the vegetable oil or butter in a pan and gently shallow fry the coated chicken, two at a time, for 5–7 minutes on each side over a medium heat. Remove from the frying pan and place on a greased baking tray. Bake the chicken in the oven for 15 minutes or until completely cooked.

Meanwhile, in another shallow pan, heat the oil for the sauce. Sauté the onion and garlic until golden brown. Add the canned tomatoes, mint leaves, garam masala, ground turmeric, chilli powder or dried chilli flakes, sugar and salt. Cover and simmer for 10 minutes.

Transfer the cooked chicken into the sauce, cover and cook for a further 5 minutes. Drizzle with a little raita and serve hot with naan bread.

CHICKEN WITH SPRING ONIONS

serves four

2 tablespoons vegetable oil

1 teaspoon cumin seeds

1 onion, chopped

1 teaspoon garlic pulp

½ teaspoon ground turmeric

2 teaspoons ground coriander

½ teaspoon chilli powder

250 g (9 oz) tomatoes, chopped

50 g (2 oz) spring onions, chopped

350 g (12 oz) chicken, cut into 2.5–4 cm
   (1–1½ in) cubes

1 teaspoon fennel seeds

1 teaspoon coriander seeds

½ teaspoon ground black pepper

½ teaspoon crushed red chillies

50 ml (2 fl oz) single cream

½ teaspoon dried fenugreek leaves

1 tablespoon chopped fresh coriander

1 teaspoon sugar

salt

chopped spring onion greens, to garnish

My family love onions and this recipe reflects their passion for them. I like to cook this when we're all spending an evening at home together.

Heat the oil in a pan and add the cumin seeds. When they begin to crackle add the chopped onion and fry for 10–15 minutes over a medium heat.

Add the garlic pulp, ground turmeric, ground coriander and chilli powder. Fry for 1 minute then add the chopped tomatoes. Continue to cook for 5–10 minutes before adding the spring onions and chicken pieces. Cook over a medium heat for 15 minutes, stirring occasionally.

In another pan dry-fry the fennel seeds, coriander seeds, black pepper and red chillies for 5–8 minutes then crush using a pestle and mortar.

Add the crushed spice mix to the sauce together with the cream, fenugreek leaves and chopped fresh coriander. Add the sugar and salt to taste.

Serve hot, garnished with chopped spring onion greens.

SLOW-COOKED CHICKEN
WITH BABY ONIONS

serves four

3 tablespoons vegetable oil

10–12 baby onions or shallots, peeled

2 green chillies, slit

8–10 curry leaves

2 onions, chopped

3 cloves garlic, crushed

1 teaspoon ginger pulp

2 teaspoons ground coriander

1 teaspoon chilli powder

½ teaspoon paprika

500 ml (17 fl oz) water or chicken stock

1 teaspoon salt

1 kg (2¼ lb) skinned chicken thighs or
    drumsticks

½ teaspoon sugar

TO GARNISH

1 teaspoon chopped fresh mint

1 tablespoon chopped fresh coriander

1 tomato, chopped

The Indian name for this dish, pyaz aur murgh ki haandi, tells you that it was traditionally made in an earthenware pot (haandi). If you don't have one you can use a slow cooker, crockpot or casserole dish.

Heat the oil in a large, flame-proof casserole dish or in a saucepan. Sauté the baby onions or shallots gently for 2–3 minutes. Remove from the pan and place on absorbent kitchen paper.

Using the same oil fry the chillies, curry leaves and chopped onions for 5 minutes, or until the onions are light brown in colour and slightly translucent. Add the garlic, ginger, ground coriander, chilli powder, paprika, water or chicken stock and salt. Bring to the boil and add the chicken. Reduce the heat and cook, uncovered, for about 20–30 minutes.

Return the sautéed baby onions to the pan, together with the sugar. Stir and cook for a further 3–4 minutes.

Garnish with the mint, fresh coriander leaves and chopped tomato and serve hot with chapattis or naan bread.

RICE WITH
MINCED LAMB

serves four

150 g (5 oz) basmati rice

50 ml (2 fl oz) vegetable oil

2 cloves

2 green cardamom pods

2 x 2.5 cm (1 in) pieces cinnamon stick

½ teaspoon cumin seeds

1 onion, chopped

1 tablespoon garlic pulp

200 g (7 oz) tomatoes, chopped

1 teaspoon ground turmeric

½ teaspoon chilli powder

4 teaspoons ground coriander

2 teaspoons garam masala

250 g (9 oz) minced lamb

2 green chillies, slit

100 g (4 oz) potatoes, peeled and diced

1 tablespoon fresh mint, chopped

1 tablespoon chopped fresh coriander

salt

FOR THE DOUGH (TO SEAL THE VESSEL)

flour, as required

water, as required

The Indian name for this recipe is dum kheema pulav, which translates as 'rice cooked with minced lamb in a sealed vessel'. A traditional mince recipe from the north-west of India, it is not as difficult to make as it sounds. Serve it hot with a fresh yogurt raita. For me, this is comfort food at its best – a one-pot dish that is perfect for cold wintry nights.

Preheat the oven to 200°C (400°F), Gas 6.

Wash the rice in several changes of water then leave to soak for 10 minutes before draining well.

Heat the oil in an ovenproof pan that has a lid and add the cloves, cardamom pods, cinnamon and cumin seeds. When they begin to crackle add the chopped onions and fry over a medium heat for 5-10 minutes.

Add the garlic pulp, chopped tomatoes and the ground spices and stir well. Stir in the minced lamb and green chillies and continue to cook. After about 5 minutes, add the drained soaked rice, potatoes and fresh herbs and mix well.

Add enough hot water to cover the rice plus a little extra – approximately 1 cm (¹/₂ in) over the level of rice. Add salt to taste. Bring to the boil then remove from the heat.

Make a thick dough using just flour and water. Roll out to a long sausage-shape strip and use it to seal the space between the pan and its lid to prevent any air getting into the pan.

Place the ovenproof pan in the oven and cook for about 30–45 minutes. Remove the dough and lid and serve the lamb hot.

LAMB IN A CASHEW NUT AND MINT SAUCE

serves four

100 g (4 oz) cashew nuts

2 tablespoons vegetable oil

2 cloves

2 green cardamom pods

2 bay leaves

½ teaspoon cumin seeds

1 large onion, chopped

1½ teaspoons garlic pulp

1 teaspoon ginger pulp

150 g (5 oz) tomatoes, chopped

2 teaspoons ground coriander

½ teaspoon ground turmeric

350 g (12 oz) lamb, cut into 2.5–4 cm
   (1–1½ in) cubes

100 ml (3½ fl oz) single cream

2 tablespoons chopped mint, plus a few
   extra leaves to garnish

1 tablespoon chopped fresh coriander

1 teaspoon sugar

salt

This dish came about by accident when I was defrosting the fridge one day and had to use up the contents of the fridge for the evening meal. Now I make it by popular demand.

Soak the cashew nuts in hot water for 2–3 hours, drain and then work in a blender to a fine paste. Set aside.

Heat the oil in a pan and add the cloves, cardamom pods, bay leaves and cumin seeds. When they begin to crackle add the chopped onions and fry over a medium heat for 8–10 minutes.

Add the garlic pulp, ginger pulp, chopped tomatoes, ground coriander and ground turmeric. Cook, stirring constantly, for another 5 minutes.

Stir the cashew nut paste into the mixture and continue to cook for another 5 minutes.

Add the diced lamb. Reduce the heat and leave to cook, covered, for 30 minutes.

Stir in the single cream, chopped mint, coriander and sugar and adjust the seasoning to taste. Serve hot, garnished with a few mint leaves and accompanied by some plain basmati rice (see page 17).

KITCHERI

serves four

400 g (14 oz) basmati rice

300 g (11 oz) red lentils

300 g (11 oz) green split lentils

2 teaspoons vegetable oil

4 cloves

1 teaspoon cumin seeds

1–2 green chillies, chopped

4–5 bay leaves

2–3 garlic cloves, finely chopped

1 onion, sliced

1 large carrot, diced or sliced

100 g (4 oz) thawed frozen peas

1 litre (2 pints) hot water

2 teaspoons salt

1 teaspoon ground turmeric

1 tablespoon cracked black pepper

1 tablespoon butter

This is a great winter dish, especially when your spirits are low and you don't want to cook an elaborate meal. It is an all-time favourite with my family! The texture of kitcheri is very like stodgy porridge, and it is best served with a spicy salad, or natural yogurt and poppadums.

Mix the rice and lentils together in a large pan or bowl and rinse in several changes of water. Drain well.

Heat the vegetable oil in a large pan and add the cloves and cumin seeds. When the cumin seeds begin to crackle and the cloves begin to swell add the green chillies and bay leaves, followed immediately by the garlic, onion, carrot and green peas, washed lentils and rice mixture, hot water, salt, ground turmeric, black pepper and butter.

Reduce the heat and cook until the rice and lentils are cooked – approximately 20–25 minutes.

GUJARATI DAL

serves four

250 g (9 oz) yellow lentils

1 teaspoon ground turmeric

1½ teaspoons jaggery or brown sugar

1 tablespoon vegetable oil

2 cloves

2 green cardamom pods

½ teaspoon cumin seeds

½ teaspoon mustard seeds

2 bay leaves

½ teaspoon asafoetida

juice of ½ lemon

chopped fresh coriander, to garnish

Opposite: **Gujarati dal**

This is one of my favourites – a good dal can really revive the spirits!

Wash the yellow lentils in several changes of water. Put in a pan with four times their quantity of water. Add the ground turmeric and boil for 30 minutes until the lentils are mushy.

Add the jaggery or brown sugar and a little salt to taste.

In another pan, heat the oil and add the cloves, cardamom pods, cumin seeds, mustard seeds, bay leaves and asafoetida. Reduce the heat. When the seeds begin to crackle pour the mixture over the cooked lentils and stir well.

Stir in the lemon juice and sprinkle with chopped fresh coriander to garnish.

GOAN RICE

serves four

500 g (1¼ lb) basmati rice

1 tablespoon ghee or salted butter

1 tablespoon cumin seeds

1 large onion, sliced

2–4 bay leaves

8–10 cloves

5 cm (2 in) piece of cinnamon stick

8–10 whole peppercorns

8–10 green cardamom pods, slightly
   opened

800 ml (1½ pints) boiling water

2 tablespoons desiccated coconut

1½ teaspoons salt

½ teaspoon ground turmeric

1 tablespoon roasted cashew nuts,
   chopped

This rice recipe is famous along the western coast of India. It combines a variety of whole spices and is served with both vegetarian and non-vegetarian dishes. The spices will not cause any harm if eaten, but they might be too strong for some tastes. Alternatively, the whole spices can easily be removed from the rice after cooking.

Wash the rice in several changes of water then leave to soak for 10 minutes before draining well.

Heat the ghee or butter in a pan and add the cumin seeds. When they begin to crackle add the sliced onion and sauté until light golden brown. Add the rest of the whole spices and sauté for a further 1–2 minutes over a medium heat.

Reduce the heat and add the drained soaked rice. Using a wooden spoon, fold and turn the rice grains gently until all the grains are moistened and coated with the butter and spiced onion mixture. The grains will start to gradually separate. At this point add the boiling water, coconut, salt and ground turmeric.

Return to the boil. Partially cover the pan and cook for 15 minutes over a medium heat.

Add the cashew nuts, re-cover the pan, reduce the heat and cook for a further 5 minutes. The water should all have been absorbed. Turn off the heat, stir the rice with a wooden spoon and serve hot.

Tip You can easily replace the desiccated coconut with 100 ml (3½ fl oz) canned coconut milk if preferred. Just use 650 ml (22 fl oz) boiling water instead of 800 ml (1½ pints).

FRIED **SWEET POTATOES**

serves four

4 sweet potatoes

1 tablespoon ghee or butter

3 teaspoons sugar

4 scoops vanilla ice cream

½ teaspoon ground cinnamon

This traditional farmers' dessert is easy to make, affordable and absolutely delectable. I love to eat it with vanilla ice cream.

Boil the whole sweet potatoes in their skins for 10–15 minutes or until cooked. Peel and cut into dice.

Heat the ghee or butter in a pan. Add the sugar and reduce the heat. When the sugar begins to caramelize add the diced sweet potatoes and mix well.

Divide the sweet potatoes among 4 serving dishes and serve hot with a scoop of vanilla ice cream sprinkled with ground cinnamon.

A special occasion means so many different things to different people – for some Christmas is the ultimate special day while everyone has different ways of celebrating birthdays and anniversaries. In India there are hundreds of reasons to celebrate, from major Hindu feast days to harvest celebrations – Diwali, the Festival of Lights, is the most widely celebrated festival. I've included some really special dishes in this chapter, from rich meat dishes to saffron-scented desserts and sweets.

special
occasions

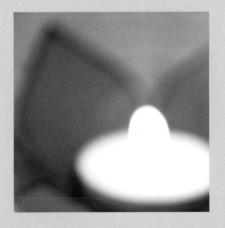

LETTUCE ROLLS

serves four

16 iceberg lettuce leaves

15 g (½ oz) butter

½ teaspoon whole cumin seeds

4 tablespoons chopped red pepper

50 g (2 oz) mushrooms, finely chopped

1 small onion, finely chopped

1 small carrot, grated

1–2 green chillies, finely chopped

½ teaspoon ground coriander

½ teaspoon salt

½ teaspoon asafoetida (optional)

2 tablespoons grated Cheddar cheese

natural yogurt, Coriander and Mint Raita
(see page 110) or sweet mango chutney,
to serve

This is a great vegetarian starter and is quite a recent innovation in Indian cookery.

Cut each lettuce leaf into a 7.5 x 15 cm (3 x 6 in) rectangle.

Heat the butter in a shallow frying pan and add the cumin seeds. When they begin to crackle add all the vegetables and spices. Cook over a medium heat for 5 minutes. Turn off the heat, sprinkle with the grated cheese and allow to cool.

Blanch the lettuce leaves in boiling water for 45 seconds. Dip in iced water, drain and pat dry with absorbent kitchen paper.

Divide the cooled vegetable filling mixture into 16 portions and put each portion on a flat lettuce leaf. Fold one long edge of each leaf rectangle towards the middle and then roll up from one short edge to make small 'wraps'.

Serve the lettuce rolls at room temperature with natural yogurt, Coriander and Mint Raita or sweet mango chutney.

HOT CHILLI SORBET

serves four

250 g (9 oz) green peppers, seeded
and chopped

4–6 green chillies, seeded and chopped

250 ml (8 fl oz) water

2 tablespoons chopped fresh mint

6 teaspoons sugar

½ teaspoon salt

TO GARNISH

unpeeled cucumber slices

sliced red pepper

sliced red chillies

Delight your guests by serving this dish between courses.

Place the green peppers and chillies in a food processor or blender, add the water and work to a purée.

Transfer the purée to a pan. Add the mint, sugar and salt and bring to the boil. Turn off the heat and leave to cool.

Press the cooled purée mixture through a sieve, pressing hard to push all the purée through the mesh. Pour into small moulds and freeze for about 1 hour.

To serve, dip the bottom of the moulds or ice cube tray into hot water to ease removal of the sorbet from the moulds. Turn the sorbet out on to individual serving dishes, arranging it on top of a slice of cucumber surrounded by long thin slivers of red pepper and chilli.

GINGERED CRAB

serves four

4 medium to large uncooked crabs

2 tablespoons vegetable oil

2 teaspoons coriander seeds

3 onions, chopped

3 teaspoons ginger pulp

3 cloves garlic, crushed

3 green or red chillies, chopped

3 bay leaves

3 teaspoons poppy seeds

2 tablespoons chopped fresh coriander

300 g (11 oz) canned chopped tomatoes

300 ml (½ pint) canned coconut milk

1 tablespoon garam masala

1½ teaspoons salt

3 tablespoons ground cashew nuts
   (optional)

This is a popular dish from Mumbai, where it is known as adraki kekda. You can use either fresh or frozen crabs – I usually go to the fish market and pick the 'fleshy' or 'meaty' ones. Indian crabs are a greyish-black in colour. Serve hot with rice, poppadums and a raita.

If you are using live crabs, blanch them in boiling water for 2 minutes and allow to cool. Remove all the meat from the shells.

Heat the oil in a deep frying pan and add the coriander seeds. When they begin to crackle and lightly brown add the onions, ginger, garlic, chillies and bay leaves.

Cook for 5–8 minutes over a medium heat before adding the poppy seeds, half the chopped fresh coriander and the tomatoes. Continue cooking for 10 minutes then add the coconut milk, half the garam masala, the salt and cashew nuts, if using. Cook, uncovered, for a further 5 minutes.

Put the crab flesh in the sauce and cover the pan. Reduce the heat and bring to a simmer. Cook for 25 minutes or until the crab meat is cooked.

Sprinkle with the remaining chopped coriander and garam masala. Turn off the heat, cover and let stand for 5 minutes before serving.

Tip The sauce can be made 3–4 days in advance and kept in the fridge. Reheat it thoroughly before adding the crab meat.

PRAWN BALICHOW

serves four

6–8 cloves

2.5 cm (1 in) piece of cinnamon stick

1½ teaspoons black mustard seeds

4 tablespoons vegetable oil

1 kg (2¼ lb) raw prawns (thawed weight
   if frozen), peeled and deveined

2 large onions, chopped

2 large tomatoes, chopped

250 ml (8 fl oz) malt vinegar

2 teaspoons ginger pulp

4 teaspoons garlic pulp

1½ teaspoons ground cumin

6–8 chopped hot red chillies

2 tablespoons brown sugar

1½ teaspoons salt

Originally called prawn balcho, this was a main dish that has now become a relish or pickle, best served with flaky parathas (see page 99).

Grind the cloves, cinnamon and mustard seeds coarsely in a coffee grinder.

Heat the oil in a pan and fry the prawns for 2–3 minutes. Remove the prawns from the oil using a slotted spoon and leave to drain on absorbent kitchen paper. Cook the onions in the same oil until translucent, about 5–8 minutes.

Add the tomatoes and cook for 8–10 minutes. Add the vinegar, ginger, garlic, ground cumin, red chillies and the ground cloves mixture. Stir and cook, uncovered, for 10 minutes.

Return the fried prawns to the pan, together with the sugar and salt. Cook for 5–8 minutes until the sauce has reduced to a thick gravy consistency.

SCALLOPS COOKED WITH MILD GOAN SPICES

serves four

20 g (¾ oz) butter

3 shallots or small red onions, finely diced

2 x 2.5 cm (1 in) pieces of cinnamon stick

6 cloves

5 spring onions, finely chopped

1 chilli, finely diced (optional)

100 ml (3½ fl oz) dry white wine

½ teaspoon salt

½ teaspoon freshly cracked black pepper

1 tablespoon double cream

675 g (1½ lb) scallops

200 ml (7 fl oz) water

2 teaspoons lemon juice

pinch of ground nutmeg

1 teaspoon chopped fresh coriander

   (optional)

The state of Goa on the west coast of India is famous for its seafood dishes. I first ate this delicately spiced dish from the northern beach huts in Goa and it has now become a firm favourite when I am cooking for a special occasion.

Heat the butter in a pan and cook the shallots or red onions for 3–4 minutes. Add the cinnamon, cloves, spring onions and chilli. Add the wine, cover and cook for 10–12 minutes. Add the salt, pepper and cream.

   Place the scallops in a separate pan and add the water and lemon juice. Simmer gently for 10 minutes. Pour the spiced onion and wine sauce, which should be fairly thick, on to a plate and add the drained scallops. Season to taste. Sprinkle with ground nutmeg and chopped fresh coriander, if using, and serve.

CHICKEN IN CARDAMOM CREAM SAUCE

serves four

2 tablespoons vegetable oil

1 teaspoon cumin seeds

2 cloves

3 green cardamom pods

2 bay leaves

2 medium onions, chopped

2 teaspoons ground coriander

2 tomatoes, chopped

350 g (12 oz) chicken, cut into 2.5–4 cm
   (1–1½ in) cubes

100 ml (3½ fl oz) single cream

2 teaspoons ground cardamom

½ teaspoon dried fenugreek leaves

1 teaspoon garam masala

½ teaspoon sugar

salt

Green cardamoms grow on small bushes, whose stems spread themselves on the ground from which the pods grow. Whenever I am in south India on a visit to the plantations in the famous Cardamom Hills, I like to get fresh cardamoms which haven't yet been dried for consumer use. This recipe, however, uses dried cardamoms, which is their most widely available form.

Heat the oil in a pan and add the cumin seeds, cloves, cardamom pods and bay leaves. When they begin to crackle add the chopped onions and fry for 5–10 minutes over a medium heat.

Add the ground coriander and chopped tomatoes and fry for another 2 minutes.

Add the diced chicken and fry, stirring continuously, for about 5 minutes.

Add the single cream, ground cardamom, fenugreek leaves and garam masala. Bring to the boil and simmer for 10–15 minutes. Add the sugar and salt to taste. Serve hot.

Tip Instead of using ready ground cardamom, you may wish to grind whole green cardamom pods yourself. Crush the pods with a pestle and mortar to crack the outer shells. The black seeds inside are the spice so remove the cracked pods before grinding the seeds.

AROMATIC SPICED LAMB

serves four

2 tablespoons vegetable oil

½ teaspoon mustard oil

2 onions, sliced

1 tablespoon garlic pulp

1 teaspoon ginger pulp

1 teaspoon ground cardamom

675 g (1½ lb) boned lamb, cut into 2.5–4 cm
(1–1½ in) cubes

1 teaspoon ground coriander

1 teaspoon ground cumin

¼ teaspoon ground nutmeg

¼ teaspoon ground cinnamon

4 tablespoons natural yogurt

1 teaspoon ground black pepper

1½ teaspoons salt

1 teaspoon sliced fresh root ginger, to
garnish

This is an authentic Hyderabadi dish eaten at festive occasions.

Heat the vegetable and mustard oils in a large, heavy-based pan. Add the sliced onions and cook over a moderate heat for about 10–15 minutes or until the onions are dark brown.

Add the garlic, ginger and ground cardamom. Cook, stirring, for 2–3 minutes. Add the lamb and all the other ingredients. Cover with a tight lid and cook until the lamb is cooked – about 30 minutes. Add a little water if the meat begins to stick to the pan.

Serve hot, garnished with sliced ginger.

LAMB IN A
CREAMY SAUCE

serves four

100 g (4 oz) cashew nuts

2 tablespoons vegetable oil

1 teaspoon cumin seeds

2 cloves

2 bay leaves

2 green cardamom pods

1 large onion, sliced

3 teaspoons garlic pulp

1 teaspoon ground turmeric

½ teaspoon chilli powder

1 teaspoon garam masala

2 teaspoons ground coriander

350 g (12 oz) boned lamb, cut into 2.5–4 cm
   (1–1½ in) cubes

100 ml (3½ fl oz) single cream

salt

1 tablespoon chopped fresh coriander, to
   garnish

This creamy lamb curry is cooked at festive occasions. The ground cashew nuts help give it a deliciously rich consistency. As an alternative garnish, sprinkle with toasted almond slivers.

Soak the cashew nuts in hot water for 2–3 hours then drain and grind to a fine paste. Set aside.

Heat the oil in a pan. Add the cumin seeds, cloves, bay leaves and cardamom pods. When they begin to crackle, add the sliced onions and fry for about 5–10 minutes over a medium heat.

Add the garlic pulp, ground turmeric, chilli powder, garam masala and ground coriander. Sprinkle with a little water and continue to cook for 2–3 minutes.

Add the cubed lamb and sauté for 5 minutes to seal the meat on all sides.

Add the cashew nut paste and mix well. Add a little water if the mixture becomes too thick and continue to cook for 20–25 minutes, covered, over a low heat.

Remove the lid, add the single cream to the curry and add salt to taste. Cook, uncovered, for 5 minutes to dry off any excess moisture.

Serve garnished with fresh coriander.

Tip Toasted almond slivers make an attractive garnish. Simply heat a cast-iron frying pan until hot and add the almond slivers. Toss the almonds for a few minutes in the hot pan, making sure they do not burn.

SMOKED LAMB
WITH **SAFFRON**

serves four

4 tablespoons milk

8–10 saffron strands

1 tablespoon vegetable oil

675 g (1½ lb) lamb, cut into 2.5–4 cm
    (1–1½ in) cubes

2 onions, chopped

2 cloves garlic, chopped

100 ml (3½ fl oz) water

½ teaspoon salt

2 teaspoons paprika

1 red pepper, cut into strips

2 tomatoes, diced

2–3 green chillies

Simple, easy and delicious, this dish comes from the southern city of Hyderabad. I sometimes make it with chicken or pork instead of lamb. Serve it with cumin rice (see page 97) or naan bread.

Heat the milk and soak the saffron strands in the hot liquid.

Meanwhile, heat the oil in a pan and sear the meat until browned all over. Remove the meat from the oil and set aside.

Sauté the onions in the same oil until translucent. Add the garlic and cook for 1–2 minutes. Return the seared meat to the pan. Add the water, cover and cook for 25–30 minutes or until the lamb is cooked.

Add the salt, paprika, red pepper and diced tomatoes. Continue cooking, covered, for 5 minutes over a medium heat.

Meanwhile, dry-fry the green chillies in a frying pan until the outside skin starts to blacken in spots. Reduce the heat and continue tossing the chillies in the pan until all the green skin has turned blackish-brown. Remove the chillies from the pan and grind them in a coffee grinder or coarsely crush or chop.

Add the saffron and milk to the meat and bring to the boil. Turn off the heat. Sprinkle the smoked chilli on to the meat. Cover and let it stand for 5 minutes, before serving.

POTATOES AND
GREEN PEPPERS COOKED WITH
PEANUTS AND COCONUT

serves four

2 tablespoons vegetable oil

½ teaspoon cumin seeds

1½ teaspoons ginger pulp

1 green chilli, chopped

1 green pepper, seeded and diced

250 g (9 oz) boiled potatoes, diced

75 g (3 oz) crushed peanuts

1 teaspoon sugar

1 teaspoon ground cumin

juice of ½ lemon

salt

**25 g (1 oz) desiccated coconut or grated
  fresh coconut**

2 tablespoons chopped fresh coriander

*This potato, peanut and coconut dish is commonly eaten by
the farmers of Maharashtra. I've given it a new twist by adding
green peppers.*

Heat the oil in a pan and add the cumin seeds. When they
begin to crackle add the ginger and green chilli and reduce the
heat. Add the diced green pepper and continue to fry over a
low heat.

  After 2–3 minutes stir in the boiled potatoes, then the
crushed peanuts. Add the sugar, ground cumin, lemon juice and
salt to taste and mix well.

  Serve sprinkled with grated coconut and chopped fresh
coriander.

MINT AND POTATO PULAV

serves four

250 g (9 oz) basmati rice

3 tablespoons mint leaves, plus extra
   to garnish

3 cloves garlic

1 cm (½ in) piece of fresh root ginger

1 green chilli

1 tablespoon chopped fresh coriander

4 tablespoons vegetable oil

3 cloves

3 green cardamom pods

3 bay leaves

½ teaspoon cumin seeds

1 onion, chopped

2 potatoes, peeled and diced

salt

Mint is not the most commonly used herb in Indian dishes but this fresh tasting mint and rice dish from the southern state of Hyderabad is wonderful served with a lamb curry like Smoked Lamb with Saffron (see page 210).

Wash the rice in several changes of water then leave to soak for 10 minutes before draining well.

Combine the mint leaves, garlic, ginger, chilli and fresh coriander in a blender and work to a fine paste. Add a little water if required.

Heat the oil in a pan then add the cloves, cardamom pods, bay leaves and cumin seeds. When they begin to crackle add the chopped onion and fry over a medium heat.

When the onions begin to soften, add the potatoes, drained soaked rice and mint paste mixture. Stir gently. Add enough hot water to come to a level 1 cm (¹/₂ in) above the layer of rice. Add salt as required and bring to the boil.

Once the water begins to boil, reduce the heat to a simmer. Cover with a lid and leave to cook. After about 15–20 minutes, remove the lid and check whether the rice is cooked. Stir once gently to avoid the rice breaking up. Replace the lid and turn off the heat.

After about 5 minutes transfer the pulav to a serving bowl. Serve hot, garnished with a few mint leaves, and with a fresh raita as an accompaniment (see page 110).

SMOKED PURÉED
AUBERGINES WITH SPICES

serves four

3 large aubergines

2 tablespoons vegetable oil

½ teaspoon cumin seeds

2.5 cm (1 in) piece of fresh root ginger,
    chopped

1 green chilli, chopped

1 large onion, chopped

2 teaspoons garlic pulp

½ teaspoon ground turmeric

½ teaspoon chilli powder

1 teaspoon ground coriander

250 g (9 oz) tomatoes, chopped

1 teaspoon ground cumin

salt

1 tablespoon chopped fresh coriander, to
    garnish

I absolutely adore aubergines – they are one of my favourite vegetables which is why I like to prepare this dish for special family occasions. It is great as an accompaniment but sometimes I also combine it with yogurt and serve it as a dip with plain poppadums.

Preheat the oven to 240°C (475°F), Gas 9.

Rub the skins of the aubergines with 1 tablespoon of the oil. Place them on a baking tray and cook in the oven for 15–20 minutes until the outer skin becomes burnt and the inner flesh is soft. Remove the skins when cool enough to handle and put the flesh in a bowl.

Heat the remaining oil in a pan and add the cumin seeds. When they begin to crackle add the chopped ginger and green chilli. After 1 minute add the chopped onions and fry for 4–5 minutes.

Stir in the garlic pulp and continue to fry. Add the ground turmeric, chilli powder and ground coriander. Sprinkle with water and fry for another minute.

Add the chopped tomatoes and continue to cook over a medium heat for 5–8 minutes.

Place the aubergine pulp on a chopping board and chop with a large knife, then stir into the spicy 'masala'. Add the ground cumin and salt to taste, sprinkle with chopped fresh coriander and serve.

Tip For an alternative dip, try replacing the aubergine pulp with an equal quantity of mashed potato.

FENUGREEK-FLAVOURED
DEEP-FRIED **BREAD**

serves four

75 g (3 oz) fresh fenugreek leaves

salt

250 g (9 oz) wholewheat flour

½ teaspoon ground turmeric

½ teaspoon cumin seeds

1 teaspoon ground cumin

½ teaspoon chilli powder

1 tablespoon chopped fresh coriander

1 tablespoon oil, plus extra for deep-frying

natural yogurt, to serve

This deep-fried bread, methi puri, comes from western Gujarat and is commonly eaten with natural yogurt. It uses fresh fenugreek leaves, which are available by the bunch in most Indian food stores. Pick the leaves from the stalk and wash them before use. Freeze any leaves left after making this recipe by drying them well on absorbent kitchen paper and freezing them in an airtight container.

Chop the fenugreek leaves, sprinkle with salt and rub in well. Leave for about 5–10 minutes then squeeze the fenugreek leaves to remove excess juices and put in a bowl.

Add the flour to the bowl together with the ground turmeric, cumin seeds, ground cumin, chilli powder, chopped fresh coriander and a little salt.

Sprinkle in enough water to make a stiff dough. Add 1 tablespoon of oil and knead well using your hands. Set aside for 30 minutes.

Divide the dough into 16. Roll out each piece on a floured board into a flat round of 7.5–10 cm (3–4 in) diameter.

Heat the oil for deep-frying in a deep pan to 180°C (350°F) then fry each puri, one at a time, for about 45–60 seconds until golden brown. Remove from the pan with a slotted spoon and drain on absorbent kitchen paper.

Serve immediately with natural yogurt.

SAFFRON SEMOLINA PUDDING

serves four

1½ teaspoons ghee

10–15 raisins

10–15 cashew nuts, roughly chopped

150 g (5 oz) semolina

75 g (3 oz) sugar

300 ml (½ pint) milk

pinch of saffron strands

slivers of almonds, to decorate (optional)

Saffron is considered the world's most expensive spice: gifts of saffron are exchanged at Diwali, the Hindu Festival of Lights and this is traditionally a dessert made on festive occasions. However, if, like me, you have a sweet tooth, you will find that you don't need an excuse to prepare this delicious dessert.

Heat the ghee in a pan and add the raisins and chopped cashew nuts. After about 2 minutes add the semolina, reduce the heat and cook, stirring, for 2–3 minutes.

Add the sugar and mix well. Pour in the milk and add the saffron. Cook over a low to medium heat, whisking well.

When the mixture begins to thicken and the semolina is cooked remove from the heat. Decorate with slivers of almonds, if liked, and serve hot.

SAFFRON-FLAVOURED
THICK YOGURT

serves four

500 g (1¼ lb) natural yogurt

100 g (4 oz) sugar

pinch saffron strands

100 ml (3½ fl oz) milk

Better than fruit yogurt, this dessert is commonly made during the summer months in India to counteract the scorching summer heat.

Tip the natural yogurt on to a piece of muslin cloth. Bring together the 4 corners of the cloth, tie them into a knot and hang the cloth of yogurt over a bowl or sink to let the excess water from the yogurt drain away. Leave overnight.

The next day tip the drained thick yogurt into a bowl and whisk in the sugar until it dissolves.

Heat the saffron and milk together in a pan and cook over a low heat for 10–15 minutes until the milk reduces and becomes dark yellow in colour. Whisk the milk into the yogurt.

Pour the yogurt mixture into 4 serving dishes. Refrigerate when cool and serve chilled.

Opposite: **Saffron semolina pudding**

NUTTY BARFI

serves four

100 g (4 oz) cashew nuts, coarsely ground,
   or ready chopped cashew nuts (very
   small pieces)

100 g (4 oz) shelled pistachios, coarsely
   ground

100 g (4 oz) almonds, coarsely ground

50 g (2 oz) desiccated coconut

2 teaspoons ground green cardamom

1 teaspoon ground nutmeg

300 g (11 oz) sugar

175 ml (6 fl oz) water

8–10 saffron strands steeped in 1 teaspoon
   hot water

200 g (7 oz) ghee

75 g (3 oz) coarse semolina

100 g (4 oz) chickpea flour (besan)

TO DECORATE (OPTIONAL)

slivers of pistachios

slivers of almonds

saffron strands

I usually grind the nuts for this recipe in a coffee grinder. This barfi keeps well at room temperature for 7 days. In a warmer climate keep it in the fridge and simply heat for 30 seconds in a microwave before serving.

Mix all the chopped nuts, desiccated coconut, ground cardamom and nutmeg in a large bowl.

Combine the sugar and water in a pan and heat until the sugar melts. Reduce the heat and simmer for 5–8 minutes. Add the saffron together with the steeping water.

Meanwhile, heat the ghee in a wok. When it becomes very hot and melts, reduce the heat and add the semolina. Cook, stirring continuously. After 10 minutes or when the semolina turns golden brown, add the chickpea flour. Cook for 5 minutes, stirring continuously. Stir this mixture into the nuts, mixing well with a wooden spoon, then add the sugar syrup.

Pour the mixture while hot into a baking tray. Leave to cool. Decorate the barfi with slivers of pistachios, almonds and strands of saffron if liked. Cut into squares and serve.

PISTACHIO AND COCONUT BARFI

serves four

4 tablespoons melted ghee

300 ml (½ pint) canned coconut milk

150 g (5 oz) full-fat milk powder

150 g (5 oz) desiccated coconut

4 tablespoons water

150 g (5 oz) caster sugar

2 teaspoons ground cardamom

6 tablespoons shelled chopped green
    pistachios

½ teaspoon ground nutmeg

saffron stands, to decorate (optional)

Like the Nutty Barfi opposite, this dessert is often made for special occasions and always during Diwali.

Lightly grease a 25–28 cm (10–11 in) baking tray with 1 teaspoon of the ghee. Heat the remaining ghee in a saucepan. Add the coconut milk and stir in the milk powder, ensuring there are no lumps in the mixture. Add the desiccated coconut, water, caster sugar, ground cardamom, pistachios and nutmeg and mix well. The mixture should be fairly thick.

Reduce the heat and continue to cook, stirring, for 5–7 minutes. Remove from the heat and empty the contents of the pan into the foil baking tray. Spread out the mixture and flatten it evenly. Smooth the top, sprinkle over a few strands of saffron, if using, and refrigerate for 4–5 hours.

Cut the barfi into squares, arrange on a serving dish and serve chilled or at room temperature.

ACKNOWLEDGEMENTS

Special thanks go to:

Lucie Morran for making it all happen and for her dedication throughout; Alison Cannon who finally convinced me to write this book; my mother, Hansa Desai, for encouraging me to learn to cook; my parents-in-law, L.G. and Shanta Pathak, for helping me to understand the intricacies of East African Indian cooking; both my grandmothers, Sumitra Desai and Mangla Desai, who loved eating and for whom I loved to cook; Julie Saunders, for typing all the recipes and generally making my very busy life less hectic; Kuntal Desai who helped with all the location shots and travel arrangements in India; John Freeman for taking such beautiful photographs for the book; Sunil Menon for his skill in styling the recipes even when India were playing in the Cricket World Cup! Roger Hammond for designing the book; the Patak's Foods New Product Development kitchen where I tested the recipes; Jet Travel in India. Last but not least, I must thank, at New Holland, Clare Sayer and Rosemary Wilkinson for all their hard work and for making the idea for the book come to life.

Everyone at Patak's, in particular those who were involved in the location photography. A special mention goes to the team at Nexus.

And last but not least, thanks to my family and friends without whom I would not have had the inspiration to write this book.

The publishers would also like to thank the following for providing props for the photography:

Abu Sandeep Gallery
55 Beauchamp Place
London SW3 1NY
Tel: 020 7584 7713

Alessi
22 Brook Street
London W1K 5DF
Tel: 020 7518 9091

Banwait Bros
75-77 The Broadway
Southall
Middlesex UB1 1LA
Tel: 020 8574 2635

Cargo Homeshops
Tottenham Court Road
London W1P 7PL
Tel: 020 7580 2895

The Cloth Shop
290 Portobello Road
London W10 5TE
Tel: 020 8968 6001

The Conran Shop
Michelin House
81 Fulham Road
London SW3 6RD
Tel: 020 7589 7401

David Wainwright
63 Portobello Road
London W11 3DB
Tel: 020 7727 0707

Graham and Green
4,7 & 10 Elgin Crescent
London W11 2JA
Tel: 020 7727 4594

John Lewis plc
Oxford Street
London W1A 1EX
Tel: 020 7629 7711

Kara Kara
2a Pond Place
London SW3 6QZ
Tel: 020 7591 0891

Liberty
210-220 Regent Street
London W1R 6AH
Tel: 020 7734 1234

Muji
Branches nationwide
Tel: 020 7287 7323

Neal Street East
5 Neal Street
London WC2
Tel: 020 7240 0135

Neelam Sarees
388-390 Romford Road
London E7
Tel: 020 8472 2410

The Pier
200 Tottenham Court Road
London W1P 7PL
Tel: 020 7436 9642

Sandy's Fishmongers
56 King Street
Middlesex
TW1 3SH
Tel: 020 8892 5788

Thomas Goode
195 South Audley Street
London W1K 2BN
Tel: 020 7499 2823

USEFUL ADDRESSES

Many Indian ingredients are available in supermarkets. For more unusual items, head for an Asian grocery store. There are also a number of websites and mail order companies which can supply fresh ingredients to your door.

UK

Asian Food Centre
175-7 Staines Road, Hounslow
Middlesex TW3 3LF
Tel: 020 8570 7346
Asian groceries and spices.

Bristol Sweet Mart
80 St Mark's Road
Bristol BS5 6JH
Tel: 0117 951 2257
www.sweetmart.co.uk
Spices and specialist ingredients with an extensive on-line ordering service.

The Curry Club
www.curryclub.co.uk
Website with many useful links to Indian food sites.

Curry Direct
Tel: 01484 842365
www.curry.direct.dial.pipex.com
Mail order supplier of Indian ingredients.

Deepak Foods
953-959 Garrett Lane
London SW17 0LW
Tel: 020 8767 7819
Indian food hall selling pulses, pastes, pickles, spices, fresh produce and breads.

Exotic Food & Spice Centre
238-240 Victoria Market
Nottingham NG1 3PS
Tel: 0115 947 0330
Sells a range of Indian spices and fresh ingredients.

Exotic Spice
Tel: 07000 785838
www.exoticspice.co.uk
High quality herbs and spices available online.

House of Raja's
12-14 Fletcher Street
Bolton BL3 6NF
Tel: 01204 532890
www.memsaab.co.uk
Sells a vast range of produce.

Indian Spice Shop
115-119 Drummond Street
London NW1 2HL
Tel: 020 7916 1831
Spices, pastes, chutneys and rice.

International Foods Store
83-95 Derby Road
Southampton SO14 0DQ
Tel: 023 8039 9750
Spices, pastes and cooking utensils.

Nature Fresh
126-128 Upper Tooting Road
London SW17 7EN
Tel: 020 8682 4988
Indian grocer stocking an impressive array of fresh produce, as well as kulfi (Indian ices), fresh tamarind, spices and breads.

Patel Brothers
187-191 Upper Tooting Road
London SW17 7EN
Tel: 020 8767 6338
A popular Indian grocer with a huge selection of seasonings, spice mixes, sauces and pickles, as well as rice and pulses imported from India.

Quality Foods
47-61 South Road
Southall, Middlesex UB1 1SQ
Tel: 020 8917 9188
Fruit and vegetables, spices and pickles.

Seasoned Pioneers
www.seasonedpioneers.co.uk
Spices, chillies and herbs on line.

The Spice Shop
1 Blenheim Crescent
London W11 2EE
Tel: 020 7221 4448
www.thespiceshop.co.uk
Huge range of herbs and spices. Also offers a mail order service.

Sunfresh
11-12 Carlton Terrace
Green Street
London E7 8LH
Tel: 020 8470 3031
A large Indian store selling both fresh produce and dried spices.

Taj Stores
112-114a Brick Lane
London E1 6RL
Tel: 020 7377 0061
Grocer selling huge bags of rice and tins of ghee. Also stocks frozen fish and spices.

V.B. & Sons
147 Ealing Road
London HA0 4BU
Tel: 020 8785 0387
A large Indian grocer selling general ingredients as well as snacks and ready-made meals.

Wembley Exotics
133-135 Ealing Road
London HA0 4BP
Tel: 020 8900 2607
Exotic fruits and Indian pickles.

Z Malik Ltd
95 Pen-y-wain Road
Cardiff CF2 3NG
Tel: 01222 499067
An Asian grocer selling a range of Indian spices.

AUSTRALIA

Arora Spices
7 Nicholson Street
Brunswick East
VIC 3057
Tel: 03 9387 5541

Delhi Bazaar
3 Murray Place, Ringwood
VIC 3134
Tel: 03 9879 7636

Spices Supermarket
27 Hampden Rd, Nedlands
Perth, WA 6009
Tel: 08 9386 1691

NEW ZEALAND

Mahadeo's Spices and Produce
14 Virginia Avenue
Eden Terrace, Auckland
Tel: 064 9 377 4553
Email: jasai@ihug.co.nz

Eastern Food Distributors
193 Riddiford Street
Newtown, Wellington
Tel/Fax: 064 4 389 2296

Asian Foods Warehouse
300 Manchester Street
Christchurch
Tel: 064 3 365 4972

SOUTH AFRICA

Datar Spice Centre
31 Ernest Road
Rylands, Athlone
Capetown
Tel: 021 637 4203
Stocks a range of Indian spices and rice.

Gorima's Spice Shop
11a The Workshop
Durban
Tel: 031 304 0990
Spices, rice and groceries.

Indian Delite
423 Longmarket Street
Pietermaritzburg
Tel: 033 3425786
Indian spices, rice and groceries.

Lalla's Spice King
84 Cottrell Street
Korsten, Port Elizabeth
Tel: 041 4512485
Spices, flavourings and condiments.

INDEX

THE PATAK'S STORY

Meena Pathak is the Director of Product Development for the authentic Indian food brand Patak's. Patak's grew from very modest beginnings and is now the number one worldwide Indian food brand – a household name, used by professional chefs and home cooks across the world.

Patak's was founded in the late 1950s by Laxmishanker Pathak, Meena's father-in-law, following his arrival in England with his wife and children. Laxmishanker experienced great difficulty in finding employment and as a means to survive, he began making and selling Indian samosas and snacks from his home. They were well received and soon he had raised sufficient capital to buy his first small shop in North London. The business expanded with the introduction of other authentic Indian products, including pickles and chutneys, and orders flooded in.

Kirit Pathak joined the family business at the age of 17. Meena herself became involved in Patak's shortly after her marriage to Kirit in 1976 when Kirit discovered her creative cooking abilities. Having trained in food technology and hotel management with the prestigious Taj hotel group, Meena had plenty of experience to offer. After a particularly delicious meal she had cooked for the family one evening Kirit asked her, 'Can you get that into a jar?', and her career in recipe and product development took off from there.

Throughout the 70s and 80s, the business prospered under Kirit and Meena's guidance. The product portfolio was extended to include poppadums and other Indian accompaniments and, in addition to supplying the Indian restaurant trade with pastes and chutneys, Patak's began exporting its range across the world into mainstream grocery markets.

Meena believes that the key to a successful Indian dish is not just the distinctiveness of the recipe but also the quality and freshness of the herbs, spices and ingredients used. Because of this, Kirit personally supervises the importation of the key ingredients from India and around the world. The

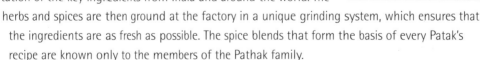

herbs and spices are then ground at the factory in a unique grinding system, which ensures that the ingredients are as fresh as possible. The spice blends that form the basis of every Patak's recipe are known only to the members of the Pathak family.

The company's range has extended over the years from pickles and chutneys, to pastes and cooking sauces in jars and cans, ready-made meals, poppadums, Indian breads and now includes Indian snacks and frozen and chilled meals.

Patak's products are now widely available, enabling consumers to produce their favourite Indian meals at home.

For more information on the company, visit the web site at www.pataks.co.uk.